PITS TO PURPOSE - WIN AT LIFE
- Instruction Manual -

PITS TO PURPOSE - WIN AT LIFE

- Instruction Manual -

JEFF BRANAMAN

XULON ELITE

Xulon Press Elite
2301 Lucien Way #415
Maitland, FL 32751
407.339.4217
www.xulonpress.com

© 2023 by Jeff Branaman

All rights reserved solely by the author. The author guarantees all contents are original and do not infringe upon the legal rights of any other person or work. No part of this book may be reproduced in any form without the permission of the author. The views expressed in this book are not necessarily those of the publisher.

Due to the changing nature of the Internet, if there are any web addresses, links, or URLs included in this manuscript, these may have been altered and may no longer be accessible. The views and opinions shared in this book belong solely to the author and do not necessarily reflect those of the publisher. The publisher, therefore, disclaims responsibility for the views or opinions expressed within the work.

Unless otherwise indicated, Scripture quotations taken from the Holy Bible, New International Version (NIV). Copyright © 1973, 1978, 1984, 2011 by Biblica, Inc.™. Used by permission. All rights reserved.

Paperback ISBN-13: 978-1-66286-935-8
Ebook ISBN-13: 978-1-66286-936-5

CONTENTS

Foreword vii
Jett Fuel Moment Explanation. xi

One. What Is Keeping You from Winning at Life? . . . 1
    1. Are You on the Wrong Team? 8
    2. Do You Have the Right Engine? 9
    3. Receive the Right Engine 12

Two. From "Way to Go" to "Way to Be" 14

Three. It's Important Where You Turn 19
    1. Turn to the Bible 20
    2. Turn It into a Habit. 22

Four. The Peace Place 27
    1. Where the World Looks 28
    2. Peace *with* God 30
    3. The Peace *of* God. 31

Five. Fast Forward. 37
    1. Don't look *at*. 38
    2. Don't look *Back* 41
    3. Focus Forward 43
    4. Is There Ever a Time to Look Back?. 46

Six. What's Love Got to Do with It? **53**
    1. What's Love? 54
    2. Get to Know Love 58
    3. God's Part 61
    4. Our Part. 62
    5. Love Is Risky Business 63

Seven. Bitter to Better **68**
    1. Words from Mayo Clinic 70
    2. Warming the Heart to Forgive 75
    3. Better Is Greater. 77

Eight. Don't Be a <u>Lone</u> Ranger! Join the Team **81**
    1. Do Life Together. 82
    2. Grow Together 85
    3. Go Together 88

Nine. Stepping out of Your Pit–Time for Action . . . **93**
    1. Ready? 95
    2. Set? 97

Ten. Ready, Set, Go! **100**

Steps to Peace with God 111
My Favorite Tools 117
Notes 119

FOREWORD

April 18, 2000, a Tuesday afternoon, Jeff and I were standing in front of a judge in a courtroom in Sedona, Arizona. We had both just gotten off work and went in just our sweaters and jeans to get married. As we joined hands and prepared to take our vows, I realized I had gum in my mouth. Jeff simply put his hand out and I spit my gum into his palm. The judge laughed and said, "I've got a good feeling about this one!" That was the beginning of a fast-paced life with many unexpected bumps along the way.

Three years later, I was sitting on the infield wall at Manzanita Speedway, counting non-wing sprint cars to see what place Jeff held in the race. He had started in fourth place on the outside row and was holding eighth place for the first two laps. On the third lap, I counted car 6, 7 ... 9, 10, 11 ... and the light went red.

"*Jeff Branaman, upside down in the fourth corner,*" the announcer called, as I started for our pit. Pops, my father-in-law, met me on the way and said, "It was a bad one." We were used to sprint cars rolling over, so "a bad one" meant exactly that. I then saw Jeff walking away from the car as the crowds cheered, and I breathed a sigh of relief. The totaled car was towed back to our pit, so badly mangled and broken that we couldn't even roll it into the trailer. But Jeff was okay.

Until the next morning.

I was awakened by Jeff crawling across the bedroom floor, trying to get to the bathroom. He was so dizzy he was sick. We went to the emergency room, where he was diagnosed with an inner ear concussion and told to take it easy for a week. He slept for three days straight, morning and night.

Two weeks later, we were on the track again. After the race, Jeff was a different person. Every week was the same. After each race, I went home with a different man, and didn't get my husband back until about Thursday. Then Friday, we raced again, starting the whole process over. We raced for six more months, not knowing how severely injured he really was. Nothing showed on an MRI or CT scan. But his brain was scrambled, and in October of 2003, Jeff pulled off the track because he just couldn't do it anymore.

Finally, in 2004, Jeff was diagnosed with a TBI (traumatic brain injury). The next three years are a blur, because he relied on me for everything. We had no guidance, no help, and no clue as to what to do. We just hung onto the Lord for dear life as we muddled our way through this injury.

Which brings us to today. Jeff and I decided that if we could help anyone through the mystery of a TBI, we would. But we expanded that train of thought, as we realized how many difficult life situations God has brought us through.

How do you "win at life" when life feels like it's against you? How do you survive your spouse leaving with someone else, your finances drained, your family deserting you, your boss betraying you, your friends abandoning you? How do you deal with the death of those closest to you, or moving away from your network of support?

It's through these experiences and more that this book was conceived. The chapters are a result of not only surviving these things but learning to win at life in spite of them.

Our desire is that as you read, you will come to know that God is for you, God is with you, and God has made a way for you, regardless of what your circumstances look like. And if we can help—well, let us know. I pray this book leads you to a closer walk with God, and sustained peace in your life.

Deanna Branaman

Jett Fuel Moment Explanation[1]

The "Jett Fuel Moment" concept (used in this manual to introduce Bible verses to each chapter) comes from the name of Jett Life Ministries, which Jeff and Deanna co-founded. The theme of the ministry is "Helping People Win at Life." When you see "Jett Fuel Moment," it is signaling that the next section you read will be the "power" statement from the Bible. It's my goal that as you read this manual, you will ultimately be led to read and study God's Word, the Bible.

Why "Jett Life"

Jett ... with two Ts has to do with the misspelling of my name in a Quarter Midget Nationals racing program when I was just nine years old. My father made the 'f's' in 'Jeff' look like 't's!' Thus, I was announced as "Jett" not "Jeff."

Later, as a young adult, I joined the Air Force and worked on the first F-16 fighter jets, and the name "Jett" stuck with me. The interesting thing is that neither sprint cars I raced as an adult nor F-16 fighter jets have reverse; they can go only forward and up. Through this I was reminded that God made humans to go forward, to get up! Even when we stumble and fall, or face temptations, trials and tribulations, Jesus wants to help us get up from the pits and keep going forward toward a full life, the abundant life that He created us to live; a life filled with purpose with Him.

Jett Life Ministries was created to help others win at life. John 10:10 says, "The thief comes only to kill, steal and destroy; I have come that they may have life, and have it to the full (abundant)."

The thief comes only in order to steal and kill and destroy. I came that they may have life, and have it in abundance [to the full, till it overflows].

- Jesus, John 10:10

CHAPTER 1

WHAT IS KEEPING YOU FROM WINNING AT LIFE?

Mario Andretti was my favorite race car driver when I was a little boy. My father took me to the Phoenix, Arizona, race shop where Mario's Indy 500 race car was worked on. On that monumental day, I was filled with excitement as I stood next to my father, taking in every inch of Andretti's white, blue, and red car. I didn't think it was possible to be more excited until Mario himself walked into the shop. I met my racing hero, I met his car owner, and … I sat in his race car. To this day, I can still remember the feel of my heart pounding in my chest as I stepped into the world of racing. That day solidified something in me that would steer the desire of my heart for the rest of my life. I knew I was going to be the next Mario Andretti.

Shortly afterward, my dad acquired a quarter midget race car and had it painted exactly like Mario's car. I was on my way to becoming a champion. Standing at a mighty three feet, nine inches, I had the jacket, I had the gloves, I had the helmet. I was cool. At the age of six, I was now a real race car driver. I couldn't wait to get on the track and perfect my skills.

I soon drove on my first racetrack, with long straightaways, tight corners and … a plywood fence all the way around. I took a couple of practice laps, and when the green flag dropped, I made it through turns one and two, and even turn three. But as I completed turn four, I heard a much louder, more powerful engine approaching. An older, more experienced driver blew by me on the inside so fast that I lost my focus, and I stuffed the front end of my new, awesome championship race car into that plywood fence. No checkered flag, no winning the race. My childhood thoughts and dreams of being the next Mario Andretti were crushed, just like the front of my car.

Winning at life can start this way for many of us. I had all the right equipment, but I didn't have the skill to use it. Sitting in Mario Andretti's car didn't make me a good driver. And I discovered something: *I couldn't win a race until I learned how to drive under challenging circumstances.* It wasn't enough to go out on a track by myself and drive in circles. There were no obstacles that would improve my driving skills. It wasn't until I was met with the challenges of a real race that I learned how to win.

Crash and Burn

"Crash and burn" is a term race car drivers and fans are familiar with. Many fans attend races to experience the thrill of highspeed accidents. As little kids, my stepbrother, Rick Shuman, and I would play with our little matchbox cars in the dirt of our backyard. We wrecked the cars just like we saw them at the real racetracks, saying, "Crash and burn!"

When I was thirteen or fourteen years old, Rick and I helped babysit a three-year old boy we called "Little Jeffrey." (His father, Lealand McSpadden, was a famous race car driver and one of the best sprint car drivers in the '70s, '80s, and '90s.) My brother and I would take little Jeffrey (awesome name, by the way!) and stuff him in a milk crate. We tied that crate to the back of our bicycles and peddled as fast as we could down the sidewalk, dragging him behind us. We then turned quickly into our driveway, causing the crate and little Jeffrey to slide across the driveway and "crash and burn" into the grass on the other side! Little Jeffrey crawled out of the flipped milk crate and yelled, "Crash and burn! Crash and burn! Do it again!"

I have my own "crash and burn" stories. I thought I was doing great as a self-made man. I believed my own grit and determination had brought me success, and no one could interfere with the plan I had for my life. Or so I thought. I didn't think I needed to change, but by the age of thirty-three, everything came crashing down. I had scared, hurt, and chased away everyone who was important to me. Family members had had enough, my wife had had enough, and I was left alone to deal with the misery I had created. I found myself on my knees at the foot of the bed in the guest room of my mother's house. It was there that a transformation began, and it was a pivotal moment as I committed my mess of a life to Jesus.

I was a new person when I met Deanna a few years later. We married, and I brought her into my racing world. I never dreamed my musician wife would love racing, and I watched in amazement as she became part of the muddy pit crew, changing shocks, rolling tires, and keeping stats. We were living the dream, traveling every weekend during the race season for the next three years.

During this time, God called me to prepare for ministry. I knew my racing career was going to end, but I didn't know when. Even though the weekends were exhausting, we loved the travel and excitement. We continued to pray, asking God to "give us a sign" if it was time to stop.

Maybe we loved it so much that we really didn't want to hear that we were finished.

The first "sign" God gave us was when we switched from racing winged sprint cars to non-wing sprints. This changed us to a new race club and raised the stakes on danger, because the non-wing sprint cars tended to flip higher and more violently. Deanna was completely against this change, but I was so excited to finally drive the car of my dreams. I tried to be sorry about the change, I really did. But I could hardly contain myself on the first practice run. This was a mean machine that I was meant to race from the beginning of time!

The next sign we ignored was that this new race club was nothing like our former group. We didn't seem to fit or be accepted, and we missed the comradery of our racing former friends. There was constant friction on the track and in the pit area!

The third sign was more obvious. After a race, we stayed the night in a Marriot hotel in Phoenix. We went out the next morning to discover that our truck, full of my race gear, had been stolen. Instead of asking God if this was our sign, we replaced all the race gear and bought a new truck. We prayed again, "God, if you want us to stop, give us a sign," even though we hadn't paid attention to the previous signs.

God often speaks like a gentle breeze, not loud thunder. It's much easier to ignore Him when He's speaking softly. We certainly didn't intend to ignore Him; we were just caught up in our own plans.

After the next race, a fan parked her car right where we needed to load our equipment. This transpired into, shall I say, a very heated argument between this woman and one of our crew members, and, of all people, my wife. While this was going on, I was dropped to my knees when a rock hit me in the face. Two kids were throwing rocks, and I happened to get in the crossfire. A member of our pit crew began yelling at the kids, which caused their large, muscled, tattooed fathers to step into the situation. With blood dripping down my face, I had to separate all these guys before someone really got hurt.

"God? Are we done with racing? Can you give us a sign?" we prayed.

The final sign was a loud thundering voice. It was the main event in a race, and I was in a strong start position. On the third lap, in the third corner, traveling about 110 mph, I failed to pitch the car sideways enough, which caused the front end of my car to jump the cushion. (The cushion is a berm of mud that separates the good racing surface from the bad area, which is also called marbles.) Immediately I was out of control as my right front tire caught the concrete wall, causing my car to flip nose to tail several times, then barrel roll a few more times before coming to rest on its side. When this is happening, you just try to keep from losing consciousness and count how many times your car hits the ground until you stop. I had crashed and burned.

I was knocked out but came to fast. I got out of the car and walked away while the crowd cheered. The car was totaled, the frame was broken, the wheels were cockeyed; it was a bad crash. I had already been dinged in race accidents a few years prior and tried to keep these injuries hidden from my wife and team members. I had never really healed from those, so this one was just icing on the old brain-injury cake.

We ended the night, and Deanna drove home. When I woke up the next morning, I was so dizzy I couldn't walk. Sick to my stomach, I crawled across the bedroom floor to the bathroom. Deanna drove me to the emergency room, where I was diagnosed with a concussion. "Just rest a few days and you'll be fine." I slept straight for three days and nights. It was hard to recover.

Two weeks later, we raced again, but I was off. My reaction time was delayed, and every time I got in the car, my head was messed up again. I tried to race for six more months before I pulled in and told my crew I couldn't do it anymore.

We finally found a doctor who would correctly diagnose me. I had a traumatic brain injury (TBI). I was a different man. I was irritable, emotional, couldn't make decisions, unstable, and frustrated. I regularly had pain radiating down my jaw, my eyes drooped, and when I was tired, I sounded like I was drunk. Our lives were changed forever.

In my first crash and burn moment, or pit of life, my heart was broken. My second crash broke my heart again, killing my dreams, and wrecking my brain.

Maybe you're in a pit now. Or maybe you began living a mediocre life instead of trying to get out of that pit. All of us certainly know others who have gotten stuck in a difficult place in life. Sometimes we find our way into the pits because of something we've done, like wrecking a race car. It could be caused by a character flaw, bad conduct, wrong words, poor planning, bad decisions, and so forth. It could be that life just happened and the mud of the world splattered on us through no fault of our own, as in an accident or health issue. Only you know. No, let me rephrase that. Sometimes we're blind to our own reality. It might take someone from the outside looking in to tell you why you've crashed. But if we want to leave a pit and really start winning at life, we need to realize why we crashed in the first place.

Part One
Are You on the Wrong Team?

What team are you on? Who's the team owner? Who's in charge? If the answer is you, or anyone other than God, then you're on the wrong team. A team without a firm foundation won't last. It will spoil like fruit you leave sitting on the counter for days. But when you choose Jesus, you have a team and owner that are imperishable. They last forever.

If you like my car illustrations, think of it this way. It's like driving a Chevy Camaro but using a Ford Mustang instruction manual to maintain it! We'll never win at this life without teaming up with the car builder. I believe that the God of the Bible created us. He's the Builder and the Owner, and He knows what works. Once we *realize* that we're on the wrong team and decide to change to the right team, Jesus will deliver us out of the pits and guide us toward the full life` He died to give us. Jesus will be the means, or provide the means, to leave the pits.

Jett Fuel Moment

There's both a perishable team and an imperishable team in this world. 1 Peter 1:17–19, 23, says, *"Since you call on a Father who judges each person's work impartially, live out your time as foreigners here in reverent fear. For you know that it was not with perishable things such as silver or gold that you were redeemed from the empty way of life handed down to you from your ancestors, but with the precious blood of Christ, a Lamb without blemish or defect. For you have been born again, not of perishable seed, but of imperishable, through the living and enduring word of God."*

Part Two
Do You Have the Right Engine?

Maybe we're not winning in life because we either have the wrong engine, or we if we have the right engine, we are only using three out of eight cylinders!

When I say the "engine," I'm talking about the heart. In Part One, I stated that we needed to realize if we were on the wrong team and had the wrong car builder. We needed to join God's team (the right car builder—our Creator).

Once we're on the right team, the car builder (God), will want to do some overhauling of our parts. First and foremost, He will want to work on our heart. We need a heart transplant if we're going to leave the pits and start winning, living a life of purpose and fulfillment.

Man, did I have the wrong engine for many years. I can't believe that I stayed alive for the first thirty-three years of my life. My parents did a great job at teaching me how to respect my elders and act right in public. But I only used those lessons to make it through school, succeed at work, and climb the corporate ladder. In the rest of life, I raged, fought, cussed, and did certain things using certain words and gestures to really get people mad. Here's a taste of what happened on an almost daily basis, which eventually led me to the pits of life.

As a young adult, I drove all over the state of Minnesota, doing insurance inspection reports. I drove fast and passed a lot of cars. Daily, I made folks in the other cars mad, which resulted in fights and near-death experiences. Once, God miraculously delivered me from sliding into a lake as I drove a corner too fast. Another time, a truck I was passing sped up to keep me in the oncoming lane as we approached a blind curve under a railroad track! I cut another guy off, who instantly pointed a rifle at me.

But the kicker was the day I passed a cement truck, and evidently ticked the driver off. He caught me at the next stop light and began hand gestures. I delayed moving on the green light, which made him even angrier. I don't think my own hand gestures of, *"Bring it on, dude,"* helped matters!

Sure enough, there was one more traffic light ahead and it turned red. He caught up with me and took my challenge. As the driver exited the cement truck and headed for my car, I noticed how enormous this Hulk Hogan of a man was! Now, God didn't bless me with size and strength. I usually depended on being angrier than my opponent to have a fighting chance. Just a millisecond of thought processing told me that I was surely going to die if I didn't get out of there. I ran the red light and saved my life for another day. In fact, I ran a lot of lights to make sure I really lost that cement truck driver!

Sounds funny now, but not so much back then. But it was these kind of character flaws that caused the people closest to me to no longer want to be around me. And those crashes sent me to the pits of life.

Can you relate to any of this? I needed a heart transplant. You might need a heart transplant, or perhaps a tune up, if you've already received a new heart. What's keeping you from winning at life?

Jett Fuel Moment

Schedule a time to read Matthew 15:1–20. In these verses, Jesus is trying to teach religious leaders and the rest of the crowd that it's not about keeping God's laws or other good laws we choose to develop and obey. Rather, it's about the condition of our heart. We're born with a tainted heart, and it just keeps becoming more perverted as we grow up in this sin filled world. The fact is we can't fix it, clean it, or replace it on our own.

In Matthew 15:8–9, Jesus says, *"These people honor me with their lips, but their hearts are far from me. They worship me in vain; their teachings are but rules taught by men."*

In 2 Corinthians 5:17, Paul refers to our heart, *"Therefore, if anyone is in Christ, he is a new creation; the old has gone, the new has come."*

Jesus died to give us a new engine (heart) with the right motor oil (blood) running through it. This ties you to the imperishable car owner (God), who causes your new engine to run right. Awesome stuff starts flowing out of the new engine, leaving character, conduct, conversation flaws behind. (See Matthew 15:19.)

With this new heart, we *believe* with the heart, *love* from the heart, *sing* from the heart, *obey* from the heart, *give* from the heart, and *pray* from the heart.

What's keeping you from winning at life?

Remember Jett Life Ministries is based on John 10:10, where Jesus said, *"I have come that they may have life, and have it to the full."*

Are you on the right team, God's team?

Do you have the right engine (heart)?

If so, are you letting God have and use all of it?

If not—prayerfully ponder Part Three.

Part Three
The Way to the Right Team:
Receive the Right Engine

Parts One and Two might have reminded some of you of that monumental day when you became a Christian by faith in Jesus Christ. For others, God may have used these first few pages to remind you how He has come after you with His love for years. Maybe you're being convicted of your sins, which are separating you from God. Do you have a tug on your life to get right with a perfect loving God? He made you and wants a relationship with you now and forever. If so, please turn to the back of this manual to read and prayerfully consider Reverend Billy Graham's "Steps to Peace with God."[2]

Taking these simple biblical steps with God can assure your entrance into that new life, putting you on the right team, and giving you that new heart you've just read about. Once you've done this, come back and finish the rest of this manual to begin winning at life.

If you're not ready yet to enter that faith relationship with God through Jesus Christ, then please, keep reading. I believe that God's universal principles, which most humans would agree are right and good for successful living, will help you as I share them with you.

CHAPTER 2

FROM "WAY TO GO" TO "WAY TO BE"

At the age of seven, while my dad was teaching me how to race a quarter midget race car, he would say, "Way to go," because I was *doing* it right.

We would go to the racetrack and practice on Saturday's when no one else was there. Dad taught me that the fastest way to get around the track was by hitting the right spots and driving smooth. I did the same thing, lap after lap, so that I would *do* it right consistently when the real race happened.

After I had practiced alone on the racetrack for a month, my dad invited two other drivers to join us, Greg and Mark Wheeler. Our dads taught us how to pass each other–the art of setting up another car to be passed—and lap after lap, we passed each other.

Race day finally came. My clearest recollection is of our days at the Glendale, Arizona racetrack. Kids ranging from age five to sixteen raced quarter midgets on a one-tenth-mile asphalt track, with eight to ten cars per race. Greg,

Mark, and I used those practiced skills to catch the competition and pass them, many times for the victory.

And our dads always said, "Way to go!"

Now listen, there's nothing wrong with my story and what my dad taught me, but I'm going to take you to the most important word when it comes to winning in life.

"Way to Be"

"Way to be" has more to do with winning than "way to go."

The world teaches us that we must *do* things to succeed in life. Think about that for a minute. Doesn't that get exhausting? If you've ever tried to *do* something to gain someone's approval, it gets old quickly. We try to please people, gain a promotion, status, or attention, because we just want to be loved and accepted. It requires *works* or *doing*!

I'm here to tell you that most people would rather *do* something in order to get something, or to climb out of a pit. That's *if* they still have the energy to attempt to climb out! There are others who are so tired of *doing* that they've given up and resorted to living the rest of their lives in the pit of mediocrity.

What if I told you a *way* to win at life that isn't about doing or going?

I guarantee that "way to be" will help you win at life. I'm speaking from twenty-seven years of experience. *We believe and become by* **being** *with Jesus.*

Many people have never learned how to invest in a relationship and try to *do* enough instead of *be* enough. That's why friendships tend to be in shambles, marriages are ordinary, rocky, or failing, kids aren't learning how to get along with their parents, work doesn't seem to be going well, and so many other relationship problem areas. People have hurt us, so we choose to avoid real relationships.

BUT ... Jesus died for our sins because He loved us so much and wanted a restored *relationship* with you and me. Being with Jesus produces a life that could very well blast you out of the pits and into a life of purpose and fulfillment. This relationship can cause you to be a new person. It can bring you new life, a new heart, new mind, new eyes, and so much more.

When I was racing cars at seven years old, here's what I knew: My dad wanted to be with me. He hated being away from me when he had to work out of town. He raised me, spent quality time with me, taught me how to race, play ball, how to work, spend and save money, how to treat people, and so much more.

Because of his love for me, I wanted to be with him too! I wanted to please him and be like him. As a little boy, the *being* together meant more to me than what we were *doing* at the racetrack!

The reason God gave us Jesus was to restore our relationship with Him. And He's so much better at relationships than even a great earthly father could possibly be. As we spend time with Him, we get to know Him and begin to put Him first. This is the start and the constant way to begin being a new person.

Start today. Re-start today.

Jett Fuel Moment

John 6:28–29: *"Then they asked him, 'What must we do to do the works God requires?' Jesus answered, 'The work of God is this: to believe in the one he has sent.'"*

We don't *do* to know and gain God's approval; we simply *believe* in

Jesus with our heart.

Philippians 3:7–8: *"But whatever were gains to me I now consider loss for the sake of Christ. What is more, I consider everything a loss because of the surpassing worth of knowing Christ Jesus my Lord, for whose sake I have lost all things. I consider them garbage, that I may gain Christ."*

We can *know* Jesus by *being* with him.

Ephesians 4:22–24: *"You were taught, with regard to your former way of life, to put off your old self, which is being corrupted by its deceitful desires; to be made new in the attitude of your minds; and to put on the new self, created to be like God in true righteousness and holiness."*

By *being* with Jesus, we start to *become* like him. We don't become gods, but Christ-like in character and actions.

John 6:57: *"Just as the living Father sent me and I live because of the Father, so the one who feeds on me will live because of me."*

We get supernatural, transforming food for our souls as we hang with Jesus, being more like Him rather than doing more for Him.

CHAPTER 3
IT'S IMPORTANT WHERE YOU TURN

In racing, the way you enter a corner has a lot to do with how you come out of it. I learned this from Ron Shuman, one of the greatest, if not the greatest, non-wing sprint car driver. As a kid, I grew up watching races every weekend at Manzanita Speedway in Phoenix, Arizona. I was already a driver, racing quarter midgets. I dreamed of the day I could race as an adult and win at Manzanita.

I finally got my chance to race on that track. I asked Ron Shuman, then retired from racing and now the race director, for advice on how to navigate the racetrack. He told me that turns one and two were built in such a way that you didn't want to turn the car as you entered the first turn. I was told to drive it straight toward the wall until I got to the center of turns one and two, and then, and only then, turn the car. This is initially hard to do since walls can be very unforgiving!

I didn't have great luck at my first race, and I ended up in the semi-main, still racing for a position in the main event. I needed to be one of the top four cars to make it to the main event that night. I was running fifth, with one lap to go, and I drove into turn number one exactly the way Shuman had told me. I blew past the fourth-place car on the outside, right at the center of the turn, and made it into the main event! I had learned to turn.

If you're going to win at life, then you must learn to turn. In this chapter, I'm going to share with you the best place to turn and how to keep making the correct turns to win.

Part One
Turn to the Bible

Peter Seeger wrote the song "Turn, Turn, Turn,"[3] and the Byrds made it famous. Most of the words were taken from the book of Ecclesiastes in the Bible. Seeger changed a few of the words to push his call for world peace, but I hope when you hear this song that you are reminded of King Solomon's words in Ecclesiastes.

Ecclesiastes is a book about the meaning of life based on King Solomon's experiences. He spoke of times when he was not in fellowship with God, but was seeking satisfaction in all the wrong things, places, people, and false gods. The end result for Solomon was this: "All is meaningless and disappointing outside of God" (Eccl. 1:2). This is from the wisest man who ever lived!

Let's just call this chapter the Jett Fuel Moment because it's all about the Bible, which holds great importance and value which God can use to get us out of a pit and take us into our purpose.

The apostle John said this of Jesus Christ: *"In the beginning was the Word, and the Word was with God, and the Word was God. He was in the beginning with God ... The Word became flesh and made His dwelling among us"* (John 1:1–2, 14). If the Word of God became Jesus in the flesh, it would be wise to *turn* to the Word for guidance.

Solomon ended his story in Ecclesiastes with this: *"The end of the matter; all has been heard. Fear God and keep his commandments, for this is the whole duty of man"* (Eccl. 12:13). We must read God's Word so we will know when to turn.

Mike Kingery, my high school friend who played major league baseball, autographed his baseball card with the Scripture, Proverbs 3:5–6. Every time I traveled to a city to watch Mike play ball, I would get another card. I wasn't interested in God in those days, so I really didn't want that "God talk" he put on those cards. But it's interesting that when my life fell hard into the pits, I was reminded of those cards. After I first asked Christ into my heart, I was led to the next turn, which was reading the Bible. I challenge you to do this today and for the rest of your life. When you have a sincere change of heart and turn toward God, you naturally become interested in His Word. Crazy how that works!

When I initially tracked down a Bible, I remembered those baseball cards. I finally wanted to read what Mike had written on them. By the time I became a Christian, some of the cards were nine years old. (I may be a slow learner.)

Proverbs 3:5–6 says, *"Trust in the LORD with all your heart and lean not on your own understanding; in all your ways acknowledge Him, and He will make your paths straight."* This verse became my motivation, my most favorite and cherished verse to live by.

Soon God put a few other mentors in my path, and they quickly turned my attention to 2 Timothy 3:16–17: *"All Scripture is breathed out by God and profitable for teaching, for reproof, for correction, and for training in righteousness, that the man of God may be complete, equipped for every good work."*

Where should you turn for guidance? To the guidebook where you learn how to win at life. So …

Are you on the right team? God's team?

Do you have the right engine (heart)? If so, are you letting God have and use all of it?

Are you *being* with Jesus rather than *doing* for Jesus?

Are you turning toward the Bible?

Part Two
Turn It into a Habit

Humans are all about habits. We go to work or school regularly, we brush our teeth, bathe, shower … well, some of us do! Some of us have developed bad habits such as alcohol or drug abuse, vulgar talk, lying, manipulating, cheating, stealing, angry outbursts, pornography … the list goes on and on.

In Part One, I spoke about how to win at life, and how it's important to turn to the Bible. Now I want to talk about establishing new habits.

Do you know what took our winged sprint car race team from a mediocre team to one of the top three teams in the Southwest? Our habits! Each week we returned from a race, washed the car, put it on a rolling cart, and stripped it down, so that every part and system could be checked and serviced.

We also kept records on every track, the engines, gears, tires, weather conditions, and outcome, which included video footage. Part of being successful in racing is not having any DNFs (Did Not Finish!). Because of our good habits, we consistently saw the checkered flag. You can't win if you don't finish!

Today is the day to start a habit. You may need to give up an old habit to invest in this new one, but it's the thing you can do. You need to get into regular daily quality time reading the Bible.

Remember, it's not about "doing" but "being." I've been known to go overboard while establishing a new habit. When starting my quiet time with God, I decided to not let anything, no matter what it was, get in the way of my set time. Even if my wife Deanna got her toe stuck in the drain of the tub and yelled for help during my quiet time, I probably shouldn't yell back, "Be there in thirty minutes! It's my quiet time with God!" **Do you get** what I'm saying?

In the Bible, Solomon is our guy. He was given wisdom from God, but he initially chose to try and live without the habit of staying connected to God. (Take time to read Ecclesiastes.) Apart from God, Solomon investigated science and could only find vain philosophy. So, he went after the habit of worldly pleasures: drinking, building, acquiring more possessions, materialism, wealth, music, and even other gods. All of it was empty. Even though Solomon made mistakes, he eventually returned to the habit of seeking God. This changed his life, causing him to become the person God created him to be all along.

It may be challenging to start a new habit, but you can make the decision to change. The Bible is called "The Truth." Jesus Himself prayed, *"Thy Word is truth,"* in John 17:17. When we form the habit of applying the truth of the Word to our lives, we find that God will reveal the following:

A. God uses the Word to sanctify us. Sanctify means to set us apart, make us holy, righteous, and Christ-like. In John 17:17, Jesus prayed to the Father for us, *"Sanctify them by the truth. Your word is truth."* The Bible sanctifies you as you study, meditate, memorize, and apply its truths to your daily life. The Holy Spirit uses these truths to make us aware of sin so we can confess and repent. God also uses the Bible to help reveal His perfect will for your life. As you submit in obedience to God's truth, you will be sanctified by it. Cool, don't you think?

B. You will still have trouble! John 16:33 says, *"In this world you will have trouble, but take heart! I have overcome the world."*

Just because you cling to Jesus and read your Bible regularly doesn't mean you won't have trouble. But it does mean that you will be better equipped to deal with difficulties that come your way. You can, however, stop the habit of causing your own trouble!

Without living and walking closely with our King, Lord, and Savior, Jesus, we can look like a deer in headlights. Distractions can pile up, despair and depression can set in. But before we became Christians, what did we do when a crisis came? What should we do differently now? You should be making a new habit of turning to the Bible. You will find answers, strength, promises, and comfort. You will learn how to know your God, hide in Him, stand *in* Him, respond like Him, and behave like Him.

Through the habit of reading the Word, you will remember what God has said to help you fight against temptations such as old or wrong thoughts. It will help you focus on right thoughts and the truth about yourself. Always remember that God is still in control, large, and in charge over your life. Don't wander off; stay *in* Christ during times of crisis. *Treasure* **the truth!**

Job (pronounced Jōbe) said that he, *"Treasured the words of God's mouth more than daily bread"* (Job 23:12).

In Psalm 199:11, David said, *"I have hidden (treasured) your word in my heart so that I won't sin against you."*

Do you treasure God's Word? Do you crave it more than food? Make it a habit to feed your mind with the Word and let it sink deep down into your heart. *Follow the Guidebook with the Guidebook Author!* Just as Solomon found a life worth living by knowing God, you too can find your purpose through the Word.

CHAPTER 4

THE PEACE PLACE

I grew up watching race cars flip as high as the light poles on the Phoenix Manzanita track. These cars would somersault into the air and clear the twelve-foot metal retaining wall, landing in the adjacent lot with the junk yard dog. Cars would even flip onto 35th Avenue into regular traffic! I witnessed several drivers die during races, but despite all this, racing is what I craved to do as a child, and it followed me into adulthood. It was a place filled with adrenaline. But for me, it wasn't a place of peace.

In Chapter 1, I shared how I crashed into a plywood fence as a six-year-old beginning race car driver. But what I haven't shared with you yet is that between the ages of twelve and fifteen, I also raced motorcycles. In the early 1970s, these bikes had loud and smelly two-stroke engines. The sound alone stole my peace. But I wanted to race so badly that I forced my way through it. Later, as a young adult, the cars I drove had similar engines, but I learned to work through it. But when the chance of a lifetime came to drive the same 800-horsepower sprint car I had watched as a kid, my peace left again. It's one thing to watch others get in these cars and drive them, but it was quite another to have my own butt strapped to the seat! It was definitely not a place of peace when I first tried it; in fact, it took several tries to reach a place of peace in that car.

Your very own backside might not be in a "peace place" right now either. Maybe you feel you've been strapped in a place lacking peace, and anticipate this same feeling for your future in an uncertain world. I pray that the rest of this chapter not only leads you to a peace that surpasses understanding, but helps you keep it, no matter what comes your way.

Part One
Where the World Looks

Let's face it, everyone is looking for peace. But how do we get it? If you don't think you need peace, just wait. Life happens to all of us. Jesus said, *"In this world, you will have trouble."* (John 16:33) Trouble finds us, generally before we make it out of grade school and certainly before we graduate high school. If you haven't felt touched by the trouble bug, then just wait; it'll certainly find you when you start working for a living, get married, or have children. This world is a peace robber. Why do you think there are so many self-help books and shows?

Deanna and I have lived in the red rocks of Sedona, Arizona, a few different times over the years. This beautiful place, once known for its western movies, is now known for its spiritual vortexes, where energy and power are supposedly found. People travel there from all over the world to search for peace and meaning.

Bell Rock is one of the more famous red rock mountains. Millions of people come each year to climb it and meditate, attempting to find nirvana. Once, in the 1990s, hundreds of people sat on Bell Rock hoping a spaceship was going to come out of the mountain and take them to a better place: A place of peace!

Others may look to spiritualists, or peace gurus. One of Oprah's team members, Eckhart Tolle, a leading spiritual guide, and new age author, couldn't find peace because he couldn't live with the "I" and the "self" of himself. He needed to get outside of himself. He claimed he found a way to have two of himself, where he stepped outside of his original self. And there he said that "he found real peace,"[4] because he was two.

Some, like Eckhart, say you should look to yourself to manufacture your own peace. I have found that the more I look to myself, the less peace I have. But when I look to God, I find that He gives an inner peace that nothing in this world can copy. Christians (those who have faith in Christ) find peace, not from self, but from God. The Bible says that God's peace is a gift from Him.

I finally got my chance to race a sprint car without a wing. Sprint car racing has two main divisions: winged sprint car racing (an air foil on top that helps plant the car) and non-wing racing. My first opportunity to drive a sprint was in the winged division. A few years later, my car owner purchased two non-wing cars. Growing up as a kid at Manzanita Speedway in Phoenix, Arizona, non-wing is what I was born to drive. My mother was the administrative assistant at Manzanita, so I was at that track every time there was a race. It was one of the meanest tracks in the country—it separated the men from the boys! While growing up, I carefully studied some of the best non-wing drivers in the country.

When I first drove a non-wing car, we asked a current driver for his help in setting up the car to speed up our potential for success. My first race was a disaster. The car felt like a bucking bronco. The race car and I were not united. It was nothing like I had dreamed it would be. But wait! We decided to ask *the builder of our car* to set it up specifically for me. He had studied my driving style as a winged sprint car driver and knew just what to do.

My next race was drastically different. The car handled like a Cadillac, smooth and predictable. I was fast and competitive immediately. I was one with the car. I went from no peace in the race car to total peace, just by *asking the car builder for help*.

It's the same with God, our Creator, and the Giver of Peace.

Part Two
Peace *with* God

People need peace *with* God and the peace *of* God!

You see, God gives peace. It's a gift. And God is peace! Yet we can't have peace with God if we avoid the critical step of reconciliation, which I spoke about in Chapter One, Part Two. We need the right engine.

If you missed it in Chapter One or need another opportunity to find peace *with* God, then here you go. I want to offer you a second chance to consider salvation through Jesus Christ, a chance that leads to life eternal, peace, joy, and a living relationship with Him. If God is calling you to turn around or to take His hand as you reach up from the pit of life, then please flip to the end of the book to read Billy Graham's "Steps to Peace with God," a simple salvation process.

Then turn back as a new Christian and finish reading the next part of this chapter.

Part Three
The Peace *of* God

Even though Jesus was going to ascend to heaven after his death, burial, and resurrection, He told His disciples in John 16:33, *"I have told you these things so that in me you will have peace. In this world you will have trouble. But take heart! I have overcome the world."*

Peace is the presence of God, not the absence of trouble. There won't be trouble in heaven, but until then, there will be trouble on earth. For now, Jesus is our peace place. I urge you to get to know Him better than any person you've ever known. His peace is our peace as we walk with Him daily, moment by moment, until we reach heaven. Let me give you an example from my experience in the bulk oil aisle of Costco.

I was an associate pastor in Newport, Oregon, and had been studying all week to preach at the evening service. My sermon was based on Philippians 4:6–7, which says, *"Do not be anxious about anything, but in every situation, by prayer and petition, with thanksgiving, present your requests to God. And the peace of God, which transcends all understanding, will guard your hearts and your minds in Christ Jesus."* This verse is about overcoming worry, anxiety, and things that steal our peace, and how to get God's peace back.

It was the Thursday before the Sunday that I was going to preach on peace. Deanna and I drove to Costco in Albany, Oregon, which was two hours from Newport. We were new to Oregon and had already made the trip to this Costco five times. We should've known our way there by then, but we had managed, each time, to get lost, even while using the GPS on Deanna's phone.

This was trip six and once again, I sensed that her GPS was taking us away from Albany and toward Salem, Oregon. I pointed the correct direction for Deanna because I knew Costco in Albany was the other way, east of the direction we were traveling. But no, she assured me that the GPS was doing its job. The longer we drove, the more familiar I became with the terrain from the previous lost trips. I lost my peace and began to get worked up.

Have I mentioned that I suffered a career-ending brain injury from racing sprint cars in 2003? And in 2009, when this event was taking place, I was still dealing with the side effects. Panic attacks and anxiety had become my new normal in life, and I had worked very hard with God to find new ways of dealing with this ramped up brain injured version of life. Days like this, and the previous five trips to Costco really sent me through the roof. But my wife makes an adventure of everything and thought it was fun being lost on the Oregon Trail again. She was laughing and enjoying the scenery that we had now seen for the sixth time, marveling at its beauty as if it were the first time she'd seen it. This did not amuse me.

We finally found our way to Costco. Remember, it was Thursday, but the parking lot was filled as if it were Saturday. That did not help my anxiety. As I entered a row to park, the lady in front of me thought she owned the world. She walked her cart right down the center of the row and had no intention of moving over until she made it to her car. I waited, anxiety rising. We finally parked and headed toward the main entrance. As we got closer, it was as if the Super Bowl had just been let out. People were flooding out, filling the entrances. Deanna and I zigged and zagged until we finally managed to get into the store. Of course, she was still laughing and enjoying the situation, just as she had been the entire trip. By this time, however, it was beginning to ruin not only my day, but would affect her too. If I wasn't careful,

I would ruin *our* day for *all* day and maybe roll it into *several* days. Know what I mean?

Suddenly, the Holy Spirit impressed upon me the sermon I had been preparing on peace. "*A peace that surpasses understanding.*" I decided to take God at His Word, and just needed a place to get alone with Him. Aha! I had it! The bulk oil aisle of Costco! No one is ever in that aisle.

I told Deanna to go on shopping without me, and that God and I were going to meet for a while in the bulk oil section. I would catch up with her when I was done. Sure enough, no one was in the bulk oil aisle, and I began to apply God's Word from Philippians 4:6–7 to this situation. First, I humbled myself and started speaking (praying) under my breath. I quoted Philippians 4:6–7, then began breaking it down word by word into three basic parts—prayer, petition, thanksgiving—just like I had planned on preaching Sunday night.

1. *Prayer* – Prayer should start with adoring God, appreciating His presence in your life, and giving Him the honor that is due Him. Humble yourself and let Him check you out (heart condition). I said, "God, You are God and I am not. I'm reminded of Your promises and how You have blessed and cared for my wife and I this week and this year." I quoted Scripture about who He is.

2. *Petition* – This is telling God our heart and what struggles we're having. I said, "God, you know how mad I am right now. It bothers me because we keep getting lost the same way every trip. We're smarter than this, God. But I also know that it shouldn't ruin my day or cause me to treat my wife badly. I need Your help. Please forgive me for the way I have acted."

3. *Thanksgiving*: I appreciated God by thanking Him for remaining in control, even though I was frustrated. I said, "God, thank You for being You. Thank You for staying in control of my life, even right now."

You must admit, most people don't like being thankful when they're mad or in a bad mood. Number three can be a tough one. But I was trying to humble myself before God and obey what His Word says to do.

I thought hard for anything and everything to thank Him for. I thanked Him for who He was, is, and will be. I thanked Him for His love and provision and, of course, for saving my soul. By then He began to soften and heal my heart. Next, I began thanking Him for my wife, the day, and the road trip. I even thanked Him for the GPS and the time alone in the bulk oil aisle! As I did this, He indeed caused the anxiety in my heart and life to vanish. The peace from heaven began to rush over me. He was faithful. I just needed to be obedient to Him and His Word.

These three steps, completed in the presence of God, with a heart that desires to obey and love Him, led exactly into *"the peace that surpasses all understanding."* Once you've tasted that peace, you remember it, and you want more and more of it.

You may say that you have peace in your life, but apart from the God of the Bible, it is not possible. The inner peace that He gives *far surpasses* any external peace you may find. I tried to find peace many ways during my first thirty-three years, and there's no comparison.

Back to the Costco story. After my meeting with God, I found my wife in the food aisle and apologized for the way I had acted. Thankfully she was quick to forgive. We then moved on with our day.

On our drive back to Newport, she said, "Oh, I never updated my phone and that's why the GPS was taking us a different direction!" Thank God that I was no longer tempted to lose my joy and peace by a faulty phone and GPS during future trips to the Albany Costco!

My friends, that's how to have and to hold the peace *of* God in your daily life.

CHAPTER 5

FAST FORWARD

There was a season while racing sprint cars when everything was just clicking. Our race cars were dialed in, the engines ran great and our set-ups for handling were so good that I was more comfortable behind the wheel than I had ever been. I was so focused in the race car that I would look past the car right in front of me and pay attention to what the cars were doing at the end of the straightaway, even as I was coming out of the corner.

One night in Aztec, New Mexico, I was once again focused forward. In my preliminary race (heat race) I was leading the competition, running a straightaway ahead of even the second-place car. I crossed under the flag stand and suddenly, I saw that there was a race car at a dead stop in the center of the corner that I was approaching. It was stopped right in the groove that I was running. There was no warning, no yellow flag, no yellow light at the end of the straightaway. I did everything I could do to avoid plowing into him. I had made many split-second decisions in my life and had lived to tell about it; surely I could miss this car.

Thankfully, I just hit his left rear tire, adding further damage to his car, but my car was fine.

After the heat race, the driver and his car owner came stomping over to my pit area. We had been friends before this moment. They let me have it with a double barrel verbal onslaught. I tried my best to apologize and told them that a yellow flag was never thrown. They didn't care nor did they believe me. I urged them to look at the video footage that our team had of the incident. They refused. As they turned to leave, the car owner told me to get my eyes checked. When I got back home that next week, I had my eyes checked! I couldn't wait to see my old friends, or new enemies, to tell them the good news. "I have 20-20 vision!"

When you leave the pits, you should focus forward to a new different-than-before life. You should focus on the One who delivered you. This "Fast Forward" chapter is going to challenge you to quickly change your focus from the pit and adjust your heart, mind, and eyes to the new, the now, and the future.

Part One
Don't Look *At!*

I want to share the importance of focusing forward and not looking back, leaving the pits of life, and heading for your purpose, which is to start winning. But first, let's talk about the word "at." Don't look *at*.

When we find ourselves in a pit or even in a rut, we tend to focus all, or most, of our attention *at* the things right in front of us. That can lead to looking down as in "down and out," and losing the hope of things ever changing.

There was a time in the early 2000's when a fellow sprint car competitor asked if I would like to work with him. Patrick Sallaway was a professional race car driver for Bondurant School of High Performance Driving in Arizona.[5] I thought that this opportunity was the next best thing to being able to race full time. I could race sprint cars with the Southwest Tour on weekends and teach others how to drive fast during the week.

During my interview, Patrick took me on a tour of the facility, and one of the cars he had me drive was the spin car. While I was driving this car in circles, Patrick said, "Don't let this car spin out!" I thought, "*This is a no brainer for me.*" I lived to go sideways in open wheel cars. I had done it off and on since the age of six! But sure enough, as I soon as I got halfway through the first corner, the car spun out. I tried the next corner and once again, I couldn't stop it from spinning out.

Patrick had me put the car in park. Then he said, "Next time, I want you to focus your eyes where you want the car to go. If you're entering the corner, I want you to place your gaze toward the end of the corner." I did this, and I stopped spinning out! If I looked *at* the front of the car or just beyond the front hood, I spun out. If I focused several car lengths ahead, I stayed in a controlled slide. Wow!

Do you see how this relates to being, and possibly staying, stuck in the pits of life?

Jett Fuel Moment

There is an occasion in the Bible where Peter walks on water. Jesus called him to step out of the boat and walk toward him on the surface of the water. Peter was focused *out* on Jesus Christ and wanted to be with Him, so he began walking on the water. But soon he noticed a storm and began feeling the effects. His focus went from Jesus to the things, feelings, and happenings around him. Fear and panic set in. Sure enough, he started to sink. Matthew 14:31 says, *"Immediately, Jesus reached out his hand and caught him. Jesus then said, 'You of little faith, why did you doubt?'"*

When looking at the circumstances and situations that face you, quickly bounce your eyes from them to the Lord. We are used to looking to ourselves or other people for help. But people can let us down and even become tired of helping us. Others may look to created things for power to overcome problems rather than looking to the Creator. A mountain, a rock, or any other thing can't save or help you, no matter how majestic they may appear. Psalm 121:1–3 says, *"I lift up my eyes to the mountains – where does my help come from? My help comes from the Lord, the Maker of heaven and earth. He will not let your foot slip – he who watches over you will not slumber."*

The Lord never slumbers, and never gets too tired to help us. We just need to focus forward, looking *to* or *at* Him for our help. And yes, He might even use another person. But let Him make that decision.

This leads us to my next point: If we don't focus *at*, then what does focusing forward look like?

Part Two
Don't Look *Back*!

To win at life and leave the pits of life, it's best not to look at our circumstances or situations for very long. In Part One, I said that we needed to bounce our eyes from those things and focus our attention on or *at* Jesus. In this part, I want to cover "Don't look *back*!" In Part Three, we'll get to the good stuff, how to *Fast Forward*.

I've always said that *real race cars don't have mirrors.* The sprint cars I used to drive didn't have mirrors. You might be more familiar with the NASCAR race cars you can see on TV most Sundays, which have rear view mirrors. Those race car drivers can become consumed with what's happening behind them and lose their focus for what's going on in front of them. We sprint car drivers don't need to focus on what the competition is doing behind us; rather, we need to work on staying close to the car in front of us and figuring out a way to pass. It's much easier focusing on a single direction. Sprint cars … Yeah!

It's the same in life. We can get so consumed with what we've done, where we've been, and what people think about us or our failures that we can barely focus on what could be ahead. On the other hand, there are others who may spend all their time focusing on past successes instead of failures, and that also renders them ineffective. People can keep us looking back with comments like:

"You'll never change."   *"You did this."*
"You'll never make it."   *"You don't know enough."*
"You have a temper."   *"You call yourself a Christian?"*
"You're lazy."   *"You can't keep a job."*
"You don't know what love is."   *"You'll never change."*
"You're too big."   *"You're too small."*
"You're too young."   *"You're too old."*
"You're a loser."

Words like this can cut like a knife. But what if it's not others who are making us regret the past, but our own thoughts and words are keeping us stuck? Do your words sound like this:

"I can't win."   *"I can't kick this habit."*
"I'm not smart enough."   *"I'll never make it."*
"I'm not cool."   *"I'm not good looking enough."*
"I'm not worthy."   *"I can't love."*
"I can't change."   *"I think they're right about me."*

I, I, I!

If we aren't careful, we'll start acting like the miserable donkey, Eeyore, on *Winnie the Pooh*! Can't you hear his negative voice saying, *"Well, okay, I guess Jesus must have been wrong when I asked Him into my heart, and He said that I'm a new creature. I don't think the old is gone, because the new hasn't come."*

Don't look back—focus forward.

When we give our heart and life to Jesus through faith, God can impress on us many truths through His Word. We must press on with Jesus daily, having a moment-by-moment relationship with Him in order to start believing the words God says about us. This is the way you began to know what He thinks about you and what He has called you to. You will learn about the plan and the purpose He created just for you.

Put a stake in the ground right now, symbolizing your commitment to stop looking back or believing the negative things spoken to or about you. Stop paying attention to things, times, or possible traumas that keep you from focusing forward.

Part Three
Focus Forward

Have you ever noticed how powerful your eyes and mind are? What do your eyes focus on? A nice car or truck? A new dress or pants? A football game or a race? Certain television shows, news stories, scrolling on Facebook, or other information sites? What are you focused on?

In Part One, I mentioned the spin car and how my eyes were focused just beyond the hood of the car, causing me to spin out. I talked about how the disciple Peter focused on the water, waves, and wind—the storm—rather than on Jesus.

In Part Two, I mentioned looking back in the mirrors like NASCAR race drivers do. We do this by focusing on our past problems, failures, things people have spoken over us, or anything else that took place in the past.

Do you know what my eyes and head were doing when I was the most successful in a race car? My head was forward and my eyes were focused three cars ahead, not just on the car directly in front of me. If there were no cars in front of me, then my eyes were focused on the next corner or the end of the straightaway.

Just like my experience with the spin out car at Bondurant School of High Performance Driving, if I didn't look ahead, I spun out every time. But Patrick Sallaway taught me to look where I wanted to go, and I never spun out!

That's a great example of what God wants us to do when we're in the pits of life and want to win. We need a single focus beyond the *at* and the past stuff of our lives—we need to focus on Jesus Christ.

Jett Fuel Moment

In Philippians 3:12–14, the apostle Paul says, *"I don't mean to say that I have already achieved these things or that I have already reached perfection. But I press on to possess that perfection for which Christ Jesus first possessed me. No, dear brothers and sisters, I have not achieved it, but I focus on this one thing: Forgetting the past and looking forward to what lies ahead, I press on to reach the end of the race and receive the heavenly prize for which God, through Christ Jesus, is calling us."*

1. **Stop focusing on past sins and failures and even past successes.** Take your eyes off them and …
2. **Cast your eyes forward.** Have eyes of faith and look only to Jesus. When you do …
3. **The power of Jesus will take hold of you.** Then you will be able to…
4. **Focus forward with your *best*.**
5. **A single, forward focus.** In verse 13, Paul says, "This ONE THING I do." No division. Don't try and live in the present and the past; press forward in your new life.
6. **Focus forward on the higher, heavenly things.** In verse 14, Paul says, "I press on to reach the end of the race and receive the heavenly prize for which God, through Christ Jesus, is calling us." In other words, give it all you've got!

Because God has created you to live in fellowship and in relationship with Him, He wants you to represent Him by living like Him. If you've placed your faith in Jesus, you are saved and have become a child of God! So, live like it! Talk about Him! Love Him and love others like He does!

We can give it all we've got anywhere that God puts us, in every season of life. We can represent Christ in our families, jobs, retirement, at school, with friends, during hobbies, and so on. Intentionally, devotedly, aggressively, and passionately focusing forward.

Part Four
Is There Ever a Time to Look Back?

Everything in this manual is to help you win at life and leave the pits of life behind. We need to leave the past in the past and focus on Jesus Christ, seeking His ways and will for our lives. Once we ask Jesus into our hearts by faith, we've been made new. The old is gone, so let it stay gone!

I love the way Pastor Robert Morris explains it in his sermon "Staying in the Word, Three Steps to Victory."[6]

> *"Christ awakens our dead spirit to life at salvation. Up until that point in our lives, our soul (flesh) was running things, using our mind (what we think), our will (what we desire), and our emotions (what we feel). The Holy*

Spirit comes to dwell inside of us, bringing the awesome privilege and presence of God."

The Holy Spirit says to our soul, "I'm in charge now!" and our soul says, "Say what?" We want to kill the desires of the flesh and bring the soul into submission to the spirit, by the Spirit. Get it? I'll say it again: the old is gone, so let it stay gone!

Next, don't let people tempt you to live in the past, or become that old person you used to be.

And last, have a single forward focus—Jesus Christ. Give Him your all and He will take hold of you. When that happens, you might as well start singing MC Hammer's song "U Can't Touch This."[7] It's Hammer-time on the old life and Hammer-time to chisel out the new life where God refines you into His image like a precious jewel.

During our time pastoring in Newport, Oregon, we became good friends with Michael and Annie Green. Michael was a commercial fisherman in Alaska, and Annie was a joy-filled Christian woman who encouraged everyone she met. Together they helped several teens and young adult women in the area. They also loved their dogs.

They came to visit us when we were pastoring in Arvada, Colorado. Dixie, an English Pointer, came with them and that dog knew there were six chickens in the yard behind us. That's all she could think about! She wanted to catch and carry those chickens to her master! Dixie was so focused that Michael had to physically pick her up at the fence and carry her back to the travel trailer. She stayed in the focused pointer position the entire time.

That's what fast forward Christianity should look like: always focused forward. But *is there ever a time to look back?* Of course there is. For positive purposes, God may take you back to a time. He brings things to our minds to bring understanding, clarity, and inner healing. He'll show you that He was there in every instance.

There's a difference when God brings our past to mind and when we orchestrate it. If we choose to focus on the past, we don't have what it takes to fully deal with it. If other people bring up old ugly memories, they might not have the right motives or abilities to help. Satan definitely has negative purposes when he brings your negative past to mind.

Learn from the past—but don't live in the past. Determine to know God's voice whether audible, inside your head, or in your spirit. Know that when you read and meditate on His Word, He begins to speak. You can even journal your prayers to Him, writing what He's speaking to your heart. As you grow in this area, He may want you to revisit your past to bring further understanding and healing. He wants to minister to your soul and give you a God-sized concept of your life. He may show you that you need to repent and ask forgiveness, laying everything at the feet of Christ Jesus and leaving it there. That's a taste of what God might do in you, if or when He takes you back to your past.

God has taken me back to quite a few things in my past, but the following story took the longest and was the most monumental of all. While I may refer to family members, I mean no ill will if any person is spoken of in a negative light; just know that they didn't stay those people. They have also had to revisit their life decisions, growing from them, and finishing life well.

It was 2007. I was in my second year pastoring my first church. Here I was, the pastor, and I still hadn't dealt with my biggest demon: anger. God had helped me overcome a lot in the areas of my character, conduct, and conversation, but He hadn't delivered me completely from anger. He wanted my participation. I was in a season of going deep with the Lord in my quiet time every morning. I always spent some of that time studying and praying about what God's Word said about anger.

God began waking me up out of a sound sleep sharply at 2:00 a.m. He would play a video in my head, showing me where my anger started. He took me back to my childhood and showed me the root of this anger, which was when my mother was divorcing my father. Dad was kicked out of the house and Mom was forced to get a job to make ends meet. When I was only eight and my brother was four, our mother took a job at a restaurant in downtown Phoenix. She would get up early and lay out our clothes, set breakfast on the table, then back out of the carport in the dark at around 4:00 a.m. She didn't know that I was awake and would scream at the top of my lungs from the second story bedroom window as I watched her back the car out to go to work. I would then cry myself to sleep. Later, she would call to wake me for school.

Thirty-eight years later, God showed me that mental video for me to understand what made me, me. I was an angry, rage-filled, capable young boy who turned into a young man. I built a survival system around myself to operate in this world so others couldn't hurt me.

But God didn't stop there. Each morning, He would wake me at 2:00 a.m. on the dot. I finally quit fighting to go back to sleep, realizing that God wanted to talk and tuned in. The next memory was when I was in the ninth grade. While on my way to Washington High School in Phoenix, two older boys rode past me on their bicycles. They hawked loogies and spit in my face. By the time I realized what had hit me, they were gone. They were bigger. Should I have turned around and taken them on? I don't know, but it only made the anger inside me grow. My survival skills grew larger as well.

Then, on another night, God showed me a memory from my time as a young adult. I had joined the United States Air Force to support my young wife and soon to be born child. I planned my enlistment, thinking that I could see my daughter Sara be born before my departure to boot camp. I missed it by five days. I was at boot camp when the call came on May 31, 1981. I heard the news of Sara's birth and the other forty-nine boot camp GIs screamed with excitement for me. But it made me so mad, angrier than ever before. Why? Because we had planned this little girl. I wanted this little girl and I wanted to be everything to her, not just a provider. I wanted to see her being born. I felt like my own country had prevented that from happening and I was hurt.

God showed me these memories as defining moments. I've shared three huge events, but trust me, there were several more that He would show me. He not only showed me my anger, but also showed me why the people in and around my life reacted the way they did. He also let me see into other people's lives to see what made them tick. He showed me the survival techniques others developed to make it in this world. Maybe they weren't right, but just like me, they were trying to manage this sinful world.

Remember when I said God may take us back for positive purposes? It's never just about us; it's about others as well. God used these 2:00 a.m. moments to help me forgive people like my mother and others, to understand them and to give them grace and mercy. God healed me and gave me a new view of those who had hurt me.

I believe that He wants to do these things in your life too. It might not be a video event like mine, but He has many ways to communicate with His children. Our part is to seek Him with all our heart, mind, and soul so He can reveal parts of our lives that He wants to heal.

Jett Fuel Moment

In Philippians 3:13, the apostle Paul says, *"But one thing I do: Forgetting what is behind and straining toward what is ahead …"*

And in verse 14, he says, *"I press on … toward the goal to win … the prize … for which God has called me heavenward in Christ Jesus."* Do you notice what's sandwiched between these two statements by Paul? Forgetting!

Paul was not racing to gain or keep his salvation, but to continue his progress, to grow more like Christ, and to serve God. His journey teaches us the following:

- Don't forget the good things from your past, but don't live in them!
- Don't live in your past successes!
- Don't live in your past failures or sins.
- There are things from your past you might not ever fully forget, but by constantly focusing on Jesus and His will for your life, those memories, possibly traumatic, should not hold you back, hold you down, or defeat you.

Don't live in the past. The good or the bad. Got it? Great.

CHAPTER 6

WHAT'S LOVE GOT TO DO WITH IT?

By now I think you know how much I loved racing. Nothing could thwart that love. At the age of eight, during a practice session in a quarter midget, the throttle stuck, and I drove that little car with the throttle wide open into the side of my father's pickup truck. I nailed the left rear tire of that truck and came to a sudden stop. I began regaining consciousness as my father was placing me in the passenger side seat of that same truck. To the hospital I went, for seven stitches in my chin. That didn't stop my love for racing, nor did the crashes on motorcycles in my teens, or the wild and crazy flips in a sprint car in my thirties.

You would think that if a guy could love something as much as I did racing that surely I could be good at loving people. Wrong! I had stunk at love in practically all other areas of my life, including marriage, parenting, and friendships, to name a few. I wanted to love and be loved but I came to realize that I didn't know one thing about it.

I'm going to drop the red flag on you right now. In racing, the red flag means stop, just like the red light at an intersection. Listen to me carefully. I have watched a ton of people during my six decades on this earth. I've watched people from all walks of life, and I have seen very few who actually do this *love* thing well. I'm going to go out on a limb and say that you might be in this camp too. Your *love* dash light might be on low or blinking red, begging you to pull over and find the answer. Please don't skip this love chapter. This is a critical piece to help you leave the pit, leave mediocrity, and head for a life like you have never experienced. You were born for this.

Part One
What's Love?

What does love have to do with going from the pits to purpose and winning at life? Everything, my friend. Love makes the world go 'round! What the world needs now is love, sweet love! People are obsessed with love; songs are written about it, television shows and movies promote it, and advertisements use love to sell products. People say, "Love you, man," or, "Love ya," to everyone they meet. You'd think with the attention that we give the word "love" that we would have mastered it by now!

I loved racing sprint cars. I loved working on them in the shop. I loved the travel to get to the racetracks. I loved race day. I loved arriving at the track and standing in line to purchase my pit pass with my fellow competitors, their families, and their crew members. Then, once in the pits, I loved the build-up leading to the race itself. I loved checking out the track surface, unloading the car and equipment, making minor adjustments, and the final nut and bolt checks. I loved wheel-packing the track and hot laps. I loved all that stuff.

But what I loved even more was getting pushed off onto the track, firing the motor, and going from idle to wide open, starting either a qualifying lap or the beginning of a race. The speed and horsepower inside the meanest race car that circles on dirt was breathtaking. I really loved that!

An 800-horsepower engine that produces 800 pounds of torque purrs like a kitten as it idles. Once you step on the gas, it turns into a roaring, raging beast of a machine. It would go from fifteen miles an hour to one hundred twenty, just like that! That's why they're called sprint cars. They didn't have transmissions, and there are no starters to add unnecessary weight.

The world seems to show love like a sprint car. I've even been guilty of the same. I recall old movies where the man and woman fell deeply in love. They were quick to tell the other how much they loved them, and they would hug and kiss passionately. But before we can even take another sip of our cola or swallow another handful of popcorn, the actress screams, "I hate you!" And the actor responds, "I hate you more!"

Before bed, my wife and I like to watch some of the old television programs. We started watching reruns of the *Wonder Years*[8] with Kevin Arnold and Winnie Cooper. Based in the late 1960s, Kevin wanted Winnie to be his middle school girlfriend. They were on again, off again. This "in love" or "out of love story" didn't happen during only one episode. It continued to happen from week to week. By season three, I was emotionally exhausted from watching this tumultuous love story. And they were just kids who turned into teens! How could I let that show grab me like that?

I think it's because, like most of us, I could relate. We've wanted and experienced puppy love in grade school and high school. Most of us dream of what love should look like as we enter adulthood. Quite frankly, I believe that all the relationships on *The Wonder Years* are a true representation of what love really looks like. It's not just about the love between a boyfriend and girlfriend; it represents love between friends, parents, in marriage, at school and work, and everywhere else in the world.

We all want to love and be loved but we can quickly find out that we can fall out of love, or someone can fall out of love with us. Sure, love can be a "Many Splendored Thing,"[9] but another song is equally true: "Love Hurts!"[10]

By the time I turned thirty-three, I had crashed and burned in life with that thing called love. In my deepest pit of life, I confessed to God that I didn't have a clue how to give or receive love. In July of 1995, I asked Jesus to not only save my life, but to show me and teach me what real love was. I needed to learn how to give it and live it. I'd say I'm probably not the only one, so let's look at what love is according to God.

Jett Fuel Moment

Have you ever seen tree sap? Have you ever seen maple syrup come from a maple tree? Deanna and I experienced that in Minnesota. It was a very cool day of learning, beginning with tapping the tree, catching the sap, and eventually tasting it. I loved it!

In English, love is the only word we use to describe love! Because the Bible was translated from Hebrew and Greek, human and spiritual love are defined by four different words. They are:
1. *Storge*: Family love, like a parent for a child.
2. *Eros*: Romantic love.
3. *Phileo*: Friendship love.

These first three take human effort. But then we have:
4. *Agape*: Self-sacrificing love.

This is a spiritual love that comes from God.

God can help us show human love, as described above, but *agape* is more like the sap (DNA) of the tree. When, by faith, you ask Jesus into your heart to be your Savior and Lord, God and the Holy Spirit begin to live in you. You then have God's DNA flowing through you. This is the only way we can love the way God calls us to love.

Agape is a self-sacrificing love and enables us to be able to love those who are difficult to love or show love when we don't feel like it. God is the source of this kind of love, which will make more sense as you continue reading the rest of this chapter.

Part Two
Get to Know Love

Love has everything to do with winning at life and pulling out of the pits. In Matthew 22:37–40, Jesus tells us to love God and love others. *"Love the Lord your God with all your heart and with all your soul and with all your mind. This is the first and greatest commandment. And the second is like it: 'Love your neighbor as yourself.' All the Law and the Prophets hang on these two commandments."*

I've shared with you that when I asked Jesus to be my Savior, one of the first things I told Him was that I didn't know how to love. I asked Him to teach me what love was and show me how to love. I began to read the Bible and pray to God for answers. After reading about loving God and loving others in the book of Matthew, I respectfully told God, "I know what you want me to do but I don't know how! I only know how to hate really well!"

God then showed me the love chapter in 1 Corinthians 13:4-7,13: *"Love is patient, love is kind. It does not envy, it does not boast, it is not proud. It is not rude, it is not self-seeking, it is not easily angered, it keeps no record of wrongs. Love does not delight in evil but rejoices with the truth. It always protects, always trusts, always hopes, always perseveres. And now these three remain: faith, hope and love. But the greatest of these is love."*

These verses, and a similar list in Galatians, are characteristics of love. As a baby Christian, I uttered out loud to God, "Lord, how do I do that? If that's love, how will I ever do those things? And how will I do those things for the rest of my life, not just for a day, a week, or three?"

The very first week after my life crash, which included my first wife wanting a divorce, practically every person important to me had left. Devastated and on my knees, I asked Jesus for forgiveness of all my sins, sincerely repented, and asked Him to be my Savior. I then asked Him to run my life.

When I went to my first home Bible study group, June Adams, who was an older woman, answered the door. With an instant bright smile, she hugged me. I mean, really hugged me! I thought, "*I could be a convicted killer and this grandmotherly stranger would still hug me!*"

One of the first Bible studies I did at George and June Adams's house was on Galatians. In chapter 5:22–23, it says, "*But the fruit of the Spirit is love, joy, peace, patience, kindness, goodness, faithfulness, gentleness and self-control. Against such things there is no law.*"

"Oh, so love is a fruit?" I said out loud to God.

Remember that I shared that the most excellent kind of love is *agape*? Well, that's the key. A deeper description of *agape* love is "purposeful commitment to sacrificial action for another." It's not kissing, you know, not just lip service.

This kind of love is impossible *until* you apply the following scripture:

1 John 4:7–12, says, *"Dear friends, let us love one another, for love comes from God. Everyone who loves has been born of God and knows God. Whoever does not love does not know God, because God is love. This is how God showed his love among us; He sent His one and only Son into the world that we might live through Him. This is love: Not that we loved God, but that He loved us and sent His Son as an atoning sacrifice for our sins. Dear friends, since God so loved us, we also ought to love one another. No one has ever seen God; but if we love one another, God lives in us, and His love is made complete in us."*

Love? Jesus Christ is the example. Remember WWJD – *What Would Jesus Do?* What if we change it to WDJD, or *"What DID Jesus Do?" God purposefully committed to sacrificial action for another because of love.* God is love, God created love, and God shows us love. We get to know His love by spending time in prayer and reading the Word. It is when we include Jesus in every moment and every day that we learn how to love agape style.

As you read your Bible, talk to Jesus. Take time to listen for His voice as you ponder His words. You'll learn to recognize His voice as He speaks to your heart. Remember that His voice never contradicts the Bible, which is the most prominent way God speaks to His children. Jesus promised that God the Holy Spirit will come to dwell in you once you've placed your faith in Him. As you read, pray, and ask yourself the following questions:

1. **What is the Holy Spirit saying to me?**
2. **What am I doing with what He is telling me?**

Getting to know the love of God is the beginning of a life changing relationship with your Creator.

Part Three
God's Part

Philippians 2:13 says, *"For it is God who works in you to will and to act according to His good purpose."* God wants to show us how to love and He also desires to help in areas such as obedience, maturity, and ministry. Agape love becomes evident in these characteristics as we allow God to work through us as He lives *in* us.

I begged God to show and explain His love to me after asking Him into my life and heart. Back then, there was a commercial showing a person taking a big gulp of iced tea on a hot day. They would then fall backward into a refreshing pool, putting a stamp on how awesome their iced tea was. When God first revealed His love to me, I had a Nestea-plunge kind of moment! I said, "Ahh, there's help and hope for me. Thanks, Jesus!"

You should also get used to praying "Help!" You'll definitely have times when you say, "God, I can't do what you're asking me to do in these love verses." But Hebrews 13:6 says, "*The Lord is my helper, I will not be afraid.*"

The first work of the Holy Spirit in our lives is teaching us how to love so we can become more like Christ. God is the One who gives us *agape* love; we can't do this without Him. Our part is to stay in Christ, just as sap stays in the tree. But that's not all. We must participate.

Part Four
Our Part

Philippians 2:12 says, "*Therefore my dear friends, as you have always obeyed—not only in my presence but now much more in my absence—continue to work out your salvation with fear and trembling.*"

Charity or *agape* love is an act of the will and is not based on how you feel or on emotions. It's a sacrificial choice on our part to participate with God by saying, "Okay, God. Here I am. I'll be the tree and you pour the sap (*agape* love) into me and out to others."

I must admit that there are times I don't want to be God's tree. I don't want to participate and obey God. But as I've matured, I have come to love and trust Him. When God wants His love directed to, on, or around another person, no matter what I feel, I stick to my commitment to God, and I show them love.

C. S. Lewis is the author of the books *Chronicles of Narnia*. He also wrote the book *Mere Christianity*, in which

Lewis says, *"Even if the person is not 'loveable' or 'likable,' we must act as if he is, and we will discover that we will actually learn to like and love him. Similarly, even if our feelings toward God may be cold, we must act as if we are sure we love Him, and we will find that our affection toward Him will actually grow and deepen."*

Make a determined decision to be a vessel of God's love. Our part is to participate by allowing God's love to flow out of us.

Part Five
Love is Risky Business!

BUT LOVE HURTS!

In his book *The Four Loves*, author C. S. Lewis said,

> *"There is no safe investment. To love at all is to be vulnerable. Love anything, and your heart will certainly be wrung and possibly be broken. If you want to make sure of keeping it intact, you must give your heart to no one, not even to an animal. Wrap it carefully round with hobbies and little luxuries; avoid all entanglements; lock it up safe in the casket or coffin of your selfishness. But in that casket—safe, dark, motionless, airless—it will change. It will not be broken; it will become unbreakable, impenetrable, irredeemable. The alternative*

to tragedy, or at least to the risk of tragedy, is damnation. The only place outside Heaven where you can be perfectly safe from all the dangers and perturbations of love is Hell."[11]

Love is giving with no expectation for getting something in return. Ouch! Will people hurt us? Absolutely. We may even experience this with even some of our closest friends and family members. But you will hurt less when you realize that God is attempting to love through you. You will heal and be asked to love again and again by God, because God *is* love.

The title of this chapter is, "What's Love Got to Do with It?" When it comes to winning at life, love is everything! *So why should we risk it and choose to love?* **Because:**

1. **We can win at life**. We can have an "alive" life, versus a dead or mediocre, at best, life.

2. **We can have a kind of love that is permanent and has kingdom-sized results**. It goes with you into heaven because God's love is eternal. There you will hear Jesus say, "Well done, good and faithful servant." People might not respond to your love on earth and may never show that they've received love from you. Others might rebuke you in your attempts to love, but your acts may be one of the steps that make it to heaven. It is then that we will know that

God used our act of love as part of a thread that led them to salvation in Jesus, changing their lives and their eternity.

But before we go to heaven, there's a reason to love that benefits us now. 1 John 4:12 says, *"No one has ever seen God; but if we love one another, God lives in us, and His love is made complete in us."*

3. **We have the guarantee of God abiding in us and His love being perfected.** I want to be a perfect lover with an audience of one. Don't you? I love being loved by God. I love loving God. I love learning more about heavenly love, and I love pleasing the God who loves me. Being an instrument of heavenly (*agape*) love is one of the biggest spiritual highs that you will ever experience on this earth. And I've been known to ask God, "Did that please you, Lord? Did that draw us closer, Lord?"

4. **Other natural forms of love will benefit from *agape* love.**

Relationships can even be repaired because of *agape* love shining out of you and me. We can have better family love and friendships. We can even have better romantic love. Philippians 2:13 says, **"For it is God who works in you to will and to act according to His good purpose."**

Stay close to Jesus. Get dirty. Get your hair messy in closeness to Him this week. That's where it all happens.

A few months ago, God spoke to me, and I quickly wrote what He said on my desk calendar. I was developing an attitude about my wife, getting mad at her because I didn't feel she wasn't loving me right. What did I do? Well, I did what most of us do. "I'll pay her back by not loving her!" I might have even let a little hate creep in. Many of you know what I'm talking about because it's happened to you, too.

Back to what God spoke to me: "*If you die loving, you don't lose.*" Live to love, even if it kills you. You will still win. If someone isn't loving you, God will make up the difference. He uses His *agape* love to touch others and cause change. Nine times out of ten, if you keep loving someone, they will respond. And remember where agape love comes from. Stay in the Spirit because the flesh doesn't have the ability to love *agape* style! Stay *in* Jesus.

Jett Fuel Moment

Again, the Jett Fuel Moment is where the truth of scripture is applied, and the power of the Word of God is revealed.

I've shared a bit of Scripture in this chapter already. It's hard not to when it comes to love. But consider one more as we end this chapter on love being risky business!

John 1:11 says this about Jesus, "*He came to that which was his own, but his own did not receive Him.*"

Jesus Christ stepped into risky business. He put on flesh and dwelt among us out of love, even while on the way to the cross. He did so to save and restore God's relationship with us. And many people, then and now, have rejected Him. But even rejection didn't stop Jesus from loving *agape* style.

There are times in all our lives that we did not receive him. But Jesus kept loving and pursuing you and I to the point that we finally stopped and turned around to repent and receive His love, entering a salvation relationship with Him. Maybe some of you are doing this as you read this manual. There's no time like right now.

So then, if we've tasted the profound love of Jesus personally, then surely we would consider risking it by attempting to love others, even if we consider them our enemies. Whether it's the one closest to you that hurts you, or an acquaintance, or an enemy, you can take it to the prayer room with Jesus. He'll hear you, minister to you, and dust you off to help you love others.

WWJD: What would Jesus do? Risk it.
WDJD: What did Jesus do? Risked it.
WWYD? What will you do? Risk it and love people.

CHAPTER 7

BRRR (BITTER) TO BETTER

There was a fellow sprint car driver that I was accustomed to passing and beating in every race. If he started in front of me, I could quickly catch and pass him without much trouble. This guy was also one of the nicest competitors on the circuit. He was an older driver at this stage of his career. In his younger years, he was a local legend and winner. Now he was driving subpar equipment, but he just loved competing. During a preliminary heat race, it's important to win or place up front to help your starting position for the main event. But any time you can get a win, you go for it. I started in the back of the pack and had passed all but this former legend. I was licking my chops as there was one lap left and I knew I could catch him. As we exited turn four to take the white flag, signaling one lap to go, the flagman threw the checkered flag instead, ending the race. The legend won and I took second. I came roaring into my pit and as luck would have it, the former legend was pitted next to me. I jumped out of my car and started yelling at my crew that I was robbed. "They never threw the white flag," I shouted for all to hear. Strutting around like a mad rooster, I made sure even the former legend knew that it was my race to win. My sweet wife grabbed my arm and directed me to our race trailer and said; "Jeff, this man hasn't won a race in years. Look over there. Look how excited they all are. Don't rob him of that joy." Deanna certainly became the voice of reason and what we jokingly call "Holy Spirit Junior!" God was speaking loud and clear to my heart. His voice was magnified inside of me and Deanna's was ringing true on my outsides. I stopped instantly and went from bitter to better! I immediately went over and sincerely congratulated him on the win.

Unforgiveness and bitterness left unchecked can get a hold on you like it did me. While still in the cockpit of that race car, I felt deprived of that one remaining lap to take the win. Like me, it will start in your mind and then flow through your entire body. You will either stuff it and blow up later like a cancerous balloon, or you will exhaust it immediately like poisonous gas. Either way, it can affect not only the targeted person, but also innocent bystanders.

Everyone needs to do the "bitter to better" check if they are going to leave the pits, stay out of the pits, and win at life. Are you ready?

Unforgiveness leads to BPFD (Bitter Prune Face Disease). Kind of like ventriloquist Jeff Dunham's famous puppet, Walter! That is a face that looks full of bitterness from too many years of unforgiveness!

"Brrr" is for how cold it feels when someone is refusing to forgive you or how cold it feels to the person you are refusing to forgive. Brrr is my word for bitterness, and unforgiveness leads to bitterness.

Please read the article below from the Mayo Clinic staff on forgiveness. Then proceed to Part One and Two to see what God has to say about forgiveness.

Part 1
Words From Mayo Clinic

Nearly everyone has been hurt by the actions or words of another. Perhaps your mother criticized your parenting skills, your colleague sabotaged a project, or your partner had an affair. These wounds can leave you with lasting feelings of anger, bitterness or even vengeance.

But if you don't practice forgiveness, you might be the one who pays most dearly. By embracing forgiveness, you can also embrace peace, hope, gratitude, and joy. Consider how forgiveness can lead you down the path of physical, emotional, and spiritual well-being.

What is forgiveness? Generally, forgiveness is a decision to let go of resentment and thoughts of revenge. The act that hurt or offended you might always remain a part of your life, but forgiveness can lessen its grip on you and help you focus on other, more positive parts of your life. Forgiveness can even lead to feelings of understanding, empathy, and compassion for the one who hurt you.

Forgiveness doesn't mean that you deny the other person's responsibility for hurting you, and it doesn't minimize or justify the wrong. You can forgive the person without excusing the act. Forgiveness brings a kind of peace that helps you go on with life.

What are the benefits of forgiving someone? Letting go of grudges and bitterness can make way for happiness, health, and peace. Forgiveness can lead to:

- Healthier relationships
- Greater spiritual and psychological well-being
- Less anxiety, stress, and hostility
- Lower blood pressure
- Fewer symptoms of depression
- Stronger immune system
- Improved heart health
- Higher self-esteem

Why is it so easy to hold a grudge? When you're hurt by someone you love and trust, you might become angry, sad, or confused. If you dwell on hurtful events or situations, grudges filled with resentment, vengeance and hostility can take root. If you allow negative feelings to crowd out positive feelings, you might find yourself swallowed up by your own bitterness or sense of injustice.

What are the effects of holding a grudge? If you're unforgiving, you might:

- Bring anger and bitterness into every relationship and new experience
- Become so wrapped up in the wrong that you can't enjoy the present
- Become depressed or anxious
- Feel that your life lacks meaning or purpose, or that you're at odds with your spiritual beliefs
- Lose valuable and enriching connectedness with others

How do I reach a state of forgiveness? Forgiveness is a commitment to a process of change. To begin, you might:

- Consider the value of forgiveness and its importance in your life at a given time.
- Reflect on the facts of the situation, how you've reacted, and how this combination has affected your life, health, and well-being.
- Actively choose to forgive the person who's offended you when you're ready.
- Move away from your role as victim and release the control and power the offending person and situation have had in your life.

As you let go of grudges, you'll no longer define your life by how you've been hurt. You might even find compassion and understanding.

What happens if I can't forgive someone? Forgiveness can be challenging, especially if the person who's hurt you doesn't admit wrong or doesn't speak of his or her sorrow. If you find yourself stuck:

- Consider the situation from the other person's point of view.
- Ask yourself why he or she would behave in such a way. Perhaps you would have reacted similarly if you faced the same situation.
- Reflect on times you've hurt others and on those who've forgiven you.
- Write in a journal, pray, or use guided meditation—or talk with a person you've found to be wise and compassionate, such as a spiritual leader, a mental health provider, or an impartial loved one or friend.
- Be aware that forgiveness is a process and even small hurts may need to be revisited and forgiven repeatedly.

Does forgiveness guarantee reconciliation? If the hurtful event involved someone whose relationship you otherwise value, forgiveness could lead to reconciliation. This isn't always the case, however. Reconciliation might be impossible if the offender has died or is unwilling to communicate with you. In other cases, reconciliation might not be appropriate. Still, forgiveness is possible—even if reconciliation isn't.

What if I must interact with the person who hurt me, but I don't want to? If you haven't reached a state of forgiveness, being near the person who hurt you might prompt you to be tense and stressful. To handle these situations:

- Remember that you can choose to attend or avoid specific functions and gatherings. If you choose to attend, don't be surprised by a certain amount of awkwardness and perhaps even more intense feelings.
- Respect yourself and do what seems best.
- Do your best to keep an open heart and mind. You might find that the experience helps you to move forward with forgiveness.

What if the person I'm forgiving doesn't change? Getting another person to change his or her actions, behavior or words isn't the point of forgiveness. Think of forgiveness more about how it can change your life—by bringing you peace, happiness, and emotional and spiritual healing. Forgiveness can take away the power the other person continues to wield in your life.

What if I'm the one who needs forgiveness? The first step is to honestly assess and acknowledge the wrongs you've done and how those wrongs have affected others. At the same time, avoid judging yourself too harshly. You're human, and you'll make mistakes.

If you're truly sorry for something you've said or done, consider admitting it to those you've harmed. Speak of your sincere sorrow or regret, and specifically ask for forgiveness—without making excuses.

Remember, however, you can't force someone to forgive you. Others need to move to forgiveness in their own time. Whatever the outcome, commit to treating others with compassion, empathy, and respect.[12]

Part Two
The "How": Warming the Heart to Forgive

As I said earlier, unforgiveness leads to BPFD and is like poison to your soul. Here's how to go from bitter to better.

In the movie *Finding Nemo*,[13] Dory sang a song to Nemo's father to "Just keep swimming," or in other words, "Don't stop." I would change this phrase to, "Just keep going." I'll explain this in a minute.

Now listen closely. Many of us have become so entrenched in a lifestyle of unforgiveness and bitterness that we've lived this way for many years. It's going to take more than self-help experts and books. It's going to take something or someone bigger than ourselves.

As we go to the Bible and to God for our answers, we will find help.

We need the One who created us to help us remove this poison called unforgiveness from our lives. We can't do it on our own. Don't forget that God's original design for us was to walk in fellowship with Him, but that was broken because of sin. Then came Jesus. God was made into flesh and did what was needed to restore fellowship for anyone who would accept His love act of deliverance. We can start and "just keep going" with God.

2 Peter 3:18 says, *"But grow in grace and knowledge of our Lord and Savior Jesus Christ. To him be glory both now and forever! Amen."*

Here are three things from the Bible that will start warming your heart:

1. **Grow in grace.** In the previous verse, the disciple Peter was encouraging the people to stay inside the favor of God's bubble called God's grace. Determine to "just keep going" with Jesus daily through prayer, reading the Bible, doing life His way, and including Him in your life, and you will be inside His grace. Grace is the undeserved favor of God, so go and grow in God's grace.
2. **Knowledge.** If you started by accepting Jesus into your heart, then *crave* to know more and to know *Him* more. Satisfy that craving. Instead of holding on to unforgiveness and bitterness, those old cravings will begin to die, and the new "Jesus" cravings will begin to wash away the poison.
3. **Increased faith**. Basically, faith is trusting God. You've got to increase your trust level when it comes to His way of dealing with people. An active faith takes action, which involves growing, knowing, and acting. You're basically going to say, "Okay, God, I'm

going to do it Your way. I can't see it working, but okay, God."

Hebrews 11:1 says, *"Faith is being sure of what we hope for and certain of what we do not see."* This walk with God is a faith walk until we get to heaven. "I don't see how it's going to work, God, but okay, I'll forgive them. I'm going to hand my unforgiveness over to you, Lord. You take care of them; You deal with them."

Now you can move on, focus on better things, and keep your walk going with the Lord. You can stay healthy spiritually and physically. Growing in grace, knowledge, and faith will increase your mercy and forgiveness toward others. It will also keep your fellowship with God open and vibrant so that He can use you and bless your socks off for His glory, your good, and the good of others.

Want some extra Jett Fuel? Make time to read Ephesians 4:31–32 and Colossians 3:12–14. And find a mature Christian accountability partner to help you with your unforgiveness.

Part Three
Better is Greater

I find it interesting that in the Gospel of Matthew (18:21–35), Jesus teaches on greatness in the same chapter that He teaches on the unmerciful servant. My paraphrase: The boss forgives the great debt owed by his servant. But that servant goes right out, and even though he was just given great mercy, he doesn't show the same mercy to the man underneath him who owes only a small debt!

We're talking about forgiveness to get rid of bitterness. So, I'm going right to the Scriptures to make some of my points.

Jett Fuel Moment

> Matthew 18:1–4, *"At that time the disciples came to Jesus and asked, 'Who is the greatest in the kingdom of heaven?' He called a little child and had him stand among them and he said: 'I tell you the truth, unless you change and become like little children, you will never enter the kingdom of heaven. Therefore, whoever humbles himself like this child is the greatest in the kingdom of heaven."*

These are big words from Jesus. He uses a child as a picture of what greatness is supposed to look like and we need to learn from that. Think about this: honor comes from humility. We need to be humble for God to lift us up. That's really not the world's way at all, is it? Nor is it what we've been taught as we grew into adulthood.

Don't get me wrong. I'm not saying, nor do I think Jesus is saying, that children are sinless. But compared to adults, children, the little ones, are teachable. They don't want much or expect a whole lot. They have faith that God will answer their prayers, and they depend on their earthly fathers to meet their needs. That's the kind of picture Jesus is painting.

The question is this: Do you want to be great? Do you want to have a great family and great friendships? Do you want to be part of a great Christian church? For that matter, do you want to be a great Christian? Well, first and foremost, you're going to have to do something. You need to choose to be connected to the Great One Himself. John 3:16 says, *"For God so loved the world that he gave his one and only Son, that whoever believes in him shall not perish but have eternal life."*

Life! That's what I'm talking about! One of the secrets to winning at life or living life to the full is living a life of forgiveness. It takes humility for us to say, "Okay, God. I give it to you."

First, remember that God calls an unforgiving heart 'sin'! Ouch! Back to Matthew 18 where the king forgave the servant for a huge debt that he could never repay. Then the servant was unwilling to forgive a small debt that another man owed him. In Matthew 18:35, Jesus says, *"This is how my heavenly Father will treat each of you unless you forgive your brother and sister from your heart."*

First, start with God, asking Him to forgive you for holding onto unforgiveness toward Him or anyone else.

Second, pray something like this: "I'm handing over my bitterness and other poisonous things inside me and I'm even handing over my unwillingness to forgive."

Jesus says that this is how we stay holy. This is how we get our joy back and stay happy, happy, happy. And this is how we become great in God's eyes. It's a life on our knees saying, "Help!" It is a life of constantly saying, "Here, Lord, take it, I don't want it. Here's the junk that I'm holding on to in my head and my heart."

That's the way we go from bitter to better.

CHAPTER 8

DON'T BE A LONE RANGER! JOIN THE TEAM

Remember the old TV show *The Lone Ranger*?[14] I'm here to tell you, "Don't be a Lone Ranger!" Even the Lone Ranger had Tonto. They grew up together, lived life together, and were trusted friends to each other.

One of my most memorable moments regarding close friends came early in my adult racing career in Yuma, Arizona. I was roaring down the back straightaway when, suddenly, the car darted toward the wall. It happened again on the front straightaway. I pulled in and explained the problem to Chuck and Jim, my crew members.

Jim stood at the front of the car in total disbelief. He said, "A bolt that keeps the front pan-hard bar on, which keeps the front axle in place, has come out!" That made the car, running at over 100 mph, dart unexpectedly toward the wall when I was supposed to be going straight! Jim was well aware of the fact that an open wheel race car was vicious and could maim or kill a driver. The thought that he, the nut and bolt checker, missed a bolt that could have possibly hurt or killed me devastated him. He vowed that it would never happen again. And it didn't. Jim was certainly a Tonto friend and teammate, as well as a Christian brother to me.

Many of us have either been taught (or learned on our own) to be self-sufficient, and we don't really want many, or any, friends to help us in life. There are also those of us who have had friendships that left us hurt, let down, or abandoned, and we think that by putting up walls, no one can ever hurt us again. "I'll make it on my own," becomes the mindset.

Have you ever stopped to think why the Lone Ranger is called the Lone Ranger when he had a friend like Tonto? Here's why: He was the sole survivor of a group of rangers killed in an ambush. Afterward, Tonto became his closest trusted friend. Tonto called the Lone Ranger "*Kemosabe*" which means trusted scout or friend. If the Lone Ranger couldn't survive alone, how on earth will you? I urge you to open your heart and mind and learn not to be a "Lone Ranger."

Part One
Do Life Together

In order to win at life, you and I need others. Just like in auto racing or sports, we need to be part of a team to win.

We had a unique race team in my sprint car racing days. My car owner, Brent Deal, hired Chuck Swearingen to be my full-time crew chief. Chuck and his wife, Jean, had previously managed the Machinist Union Indy car team. They brought that same professional mentality to our team. As their driver, they spoiled me rotten. They ensured my travel to the tracks was paid, plus entry fees, motels, and food. They made sure half the purse money was mine. Chuck and Brent were so loyal that they never thought anything that happened on the track was my fault! Crazy! (That had to be a God thing!)

Chuck passed away from cancer in the middle of my career, and my father became the crew chief. Dad had trained me to race at age six, so it was great having him help me finish my racing career. We were finally living the dream that we both thought my adult years would bring.

Our primary team consisted of three men and three women. As we traveled together, our teamwork, roles, and unity made for great success on the track. My team was awesome, and those years were some of the most memorable times of my life. We were successful and had a great time together. Lone Ranger race car drivers don't do very well and Lone Ranger Christians don't either. There's really no such thing as a Lone Ranger Christian. You can't walk with Jesus alone. Why? Because God said so. I'll show you in the Jett Fuel Moment in a minute.

I used to say, "If I ever go to church, it won't be that one! Not Verde Baptist in Cottonwood, Arizona." So where did God take me when I was in the deepest pit of my life? Yep, Verde Baptist! Guess who became some of my closest friends? The people who attended that church whom I had previously never given the time of day.

And that's where I met Jim Ayers, the former pastor, who became a vital part of my race team. John Mahon, a bold Christian, became the accountant for the family business. Prior to this, I remember the day I was drinking a beer at the county fair when John came walking around the corner. For some reason, I felt compelled to hide the beer behind my back. I now know that it wasn't John but the presence of the Holy Spirit in him that made me want to hide my beer. John became the first person to not only teach me the Bible, but to teach me how to walk with Jesus in my new faith. And lo and behold, John and his wife, Paula, attended the church that I swore I would never go to!

I've had a healthy life together with these guys and many more just like them. Don't try to be a Lone Ranger. And don't fight God on this one, folks.

Jett Fuel Moment

God wants us to *do* life together. Acts 2:42 says, *"They devoted themselves to fellowship."* That's how things began right after Jesus ascended to heaven, and that's how God desires His children to live now.

He wants us to live in fellowship, partnering and participating with each other and sharing all things in common.

In Romans 1:11–12, the apostle Paul said, *"I long to see you that I may impart to you some spiritual gift to make you strong—that is, that you and I may be mutually encouraged by each other's faith."*

We need to be encouraged and built up. We need to worship God together. This includes eating, playing, resting, and checking on each other. We need to be together, encouraging joint participation.

If you're a Christian, you need to participate in life together with other Christians. It's the way God designed us and the way He wants His children and His family to live life. It's the way He's going to help you win at life and take you from the pits to His purpose. Other Christians can teach you how to live the full and abundant life that Jesus died for and rose again to give us.

Be sure to look for some mature, healthy Christians to *do* life with.

Start today. This week. This Sunday.

Part Two
Grow Together

As I told you, when I was thirty-three years old, I landed in a rock-bottom pit of life. I reached out to Jesus for help and asked Him to forgive me of all my sins, both against Him and others. I then asked Him into my heart and confessed with my mouth that He was my Savior and Lord.

I immediately started going to a church I said I would never attend, which I mentioned earlier. The next week, I started attending my first small group home Bible Study, led by George and June Adams, an older couple whom I had never met before.

George was a man in his late seventies. I would later learn that George had had a major pit moment early in his life and marriage. He too had character flaws like mine that he had to realize and surrender to God. George, in his seventies, still looked like a giant bear with silver hair. But he was a soft-spoken, humble man, and the love of Jesus flowed from him nonstop. He offered to meet with me alone, before and after the weekly small group study. I asked him countless questions about Jesus and the Bible, and I began to learn how to live this new Christian life. George and his wife, June, taught me how to study my Bible, how to pray, how to listen, and how to act on what God was speaking to me.

Remember the Christian business accountant that I mentioned previously? (The guy that I tried to hide my beer from?) John Mahon was the one who urged me to attend the small group. He was another person that I met with regularly. I'd say we met weekly for the first four years of my walk with Jesus. If you can imagine Jesus dangling a saving rope from heaven for us to hang on to and think of a secondary rope coming off the main rope. John was that secondary rope for me. I would try to live a new life during the week, and when a trial or a temptation would come up, I would run to John's place of business. I needed him to tell me what the Bible said about each situation. At times, we met for a fast lunch, or at his barn after work. John was available by phone or in person to help me grow in my faith and I learned how to apply his lessons in everyday life.

I raced sprint cars during this season of life. We worked in the race shop weekly and traveled on the weekends to the tracks throughout the southwest. My pastor friend Jim Ayers walked side by side with me. Whether it was at the races or in a motel, Jim not only helped me learn how to live a new life in Christ, but also brought prayer and support to myself and the team. When I was home, I met weekly at 6:00 a.m. with Harvey Cox, a Navigator missionary, learning how to develop my quiet time with the Lord.

Not only did I do all that is mentioned above, but I was also in church every time the doors were open. Sunday school, Sunday worship service, Sunday night service … even serving the teen group on Wednesday nights.

The term I gave to myself in my new life was "Jesus Geek." This was the same derogatory term I had previously called the Christians who seemed so different from the world I formerly lived in. Yet now I took that title and proudly put it on my life. I was *growing* in my faith and knowledge of Jesus, learning how He wanted me to live my life; a full, abundant life. The people I mentioned were also growing. We were a team! I was surrounded and saturated with the Lord through His family. We were all becoming more like Jesus.

Jett Fuel Moment

> Acts 2:46 says, *"Every day they continued to meet together in the temple courts. They broke bread in their homes and ate together with glad and sincere hearts."*

God causes transformational growth in His children as they gather with Him as their focus. They gathered:

In the temple: The church building, gathering for corporate worship.

In homes: Small groups, one on one.

In fellowship: They ate together and were devoted to one another.

They were united, they served, they shared, and they prayed together. (Read Acts 2:42–47 for the entire story.)

What are you doing to grow your relationship with Jesus Christ? What are you doing to grow together with other Christians?

Start now. Re-start now.

Part Three
Go Together

Henry Blackaby wrote a popular book called *Experiencing God*. His greatest line in the book is this: "Find where God is working and join Him there."[15]

When we do as the Bible says and "*Go,*" we are serving others. If you haven't really served others before, it's much easier if you "go" or "do" with others.

Take time to read Acts 2:42–47 again. The words, "they," "their," "all" and "together" are used in these verses. The apostles and the new Christians were in the center where God was working, and this scripture finishes with, "And the Lord added to their number all that were being saved."

"*Go*" is about telling and teaching others. You've probably heard of the Great Commandment, which is in Matthew 28:19–20: *"Then Jesus came to them and said, 'All authority in heaven and earth has been given to me. Therefore, GO and make disciples of all nations, baptizing them in the name of the Father and of the Son and of the Holy Spirit, and teaching them to obey everything I have commanded you"* (emphasis mine).

Jesus is very serious about us telling others what, why, how, and now of the Good News. We are to tell others what Jesus did out of love to save us by giving His life. He did this because mankind was (and is) separated from God because of sin. The how and now is that Jesus then told His followers to "Go." He said," Get out there and tell the world how to know *me*. Then teach them how to walk with God so they can *go* and do the same."

As a new Christian in my first church, I was invited to go with my new friends to help others. First, they invited me to help at the Christian school fund raiser. Second, I helped the homeless at the Old Town Mission once a month. Third, they invited me to join them in special prayer meetings.

One meeting was for a woman dealing with cancer. But as a new Christian, I didn't open my mouth when the people gathered around this woman to pray. But I prayed under my breath for her as the others prayed out loud. I agreed with their prayers. It took about a year for me to pray out loud for people. I began to see needs around me in my own life circles and asked others to help me as I served these people and their needs. By living my life together with other mature Christians, I watched as they talked to people about the Good News. They would lead them to Jesus, and teach them, just as they had taught me.

If you're a Christian, then you're called to love, serve, and share the Good News. None of us are off the hook. I initially tried to excuse myself of the share and prayer parts by telling God that I was a D-minus student in English and speech class, but He didn't seem to care! But because I believed and accepted Him, I was *compelled* to *go* with others and love, serve, share, tell, and teach. And one day, I was called by God to prepare for the ministry so that He could use me to pastor and preach. D-Minus Jeff with a brain injury from racing sprint cars was called by God to pastor! Isn't He marvelous?

Are you compelled to go together with others to share the Gospel of Jesus? I pray that you will listen to the nudge of the Holy Spirit living inside you and *go*. Join fellow Christians and find where God is working and join Him there.

Jett Fuel Moment

Acts 1:8 is considered the theme verse for the book of Acts in the Bible. *"Jesus said to themishhhh, "You will receive power when the Holy Spirit comes on you; and you will be my witnesses in Jerusalem, and in all Judea and Samaria, and to the ends of the earth."*

Going together with others is what I've been talking about. Can you imagine being given this heavenly power from God? This was the power given to the *church* to proclaim the gospel and to continue Jesus' ministry everywhere. The word "church" doesn't refer to a building, but it's the "called out assembly." Believers are the body of Christ, equipped with the power of the Holy Spirit living in us, empowering us to share the saving message of Jesus. Why would we want to do this alone? It's like acquiring the best race car engine on the planet and choosing to leave the race team at home! Sure, someone might push you onto the track for the race but how fast can you go if the tires aren't properly inflated, the right gear isn't installed, and fuel isn't in the tank? Are you getting the picture?

The book of Acts is the real-life account of the *works* of the Holy Spirit through the *acts* of the apostles and other believers. As you read the book of Acts, you will see the words, "we," "them" and "they." Seldom did the apostles go alone, but if they did, there were others praying, watching, and caring for them until they reached their destination or returned to the body.

There was persecution in the first church, just as there can be today. The result of that persecution was a scattering of the believers. Acts 8:4 states that *"Those who had been scattered preached the word wherever they went."* Do you notice the words "those" and "they"? Even though there was a scattering that reduced the mass, the fact remains that they didn't scatter into isolation. A few went this way and others went that way; to Judea, to Samaria, and eventually to the ends of the earth. They worked together to spread the gospel of Christ to the world.

We also need to go together, spreading the gospel to a world that needs Jesus more now than ever before.

CHAPTER 9

STEPPING OUT OF YOUR PIT—TIME FOR ACTION

The infield of a racetrack is called the pits. When we would get to the racetrack, my crew and I unloaded the car into our pit, along with all the tools and spare equipment. The crew did some last-minute inspections on the car as I prepped myself mentally. I then donned my fireproof race suit, shoes, gloves, helmet, and arm restraints. Once I was strapped into the car, I was pushed onto the track because I was ready to do what we came there to do: Win the race.

Prior to this though, my car owner, crew chief, and other team members had worked throughout the week on the car. Every Sunday afternoon after a race, the car was unloaded and washed. It was then lifted onto a stand and dismantled. The fuel system was purged, the oil was drained, and the motor was inspected. Every moving part that affected the handling and suspension of the car was removed and inspected. By midweek, the team was putting it all back together again. The engine was fired, and everything was double checked before it was loaded into the trailer for the next weekend of races. We were ready.

What always baffled me was hearing about fellow competitors waiting until the last minute to check their race cars. They would rush on a Thursday night to get their cars ready, hoping everything worked right at the track! Many of these racers had problems and oftentimes had DNFs ("Did Not Finish!"). They never saw the checkered flag at the end of the race.

I don't claim to be the sharpest tool in the toolbox, and I often joke about having an IQ of about fifty-six. But one thing I got early on: If you don't finish the race, you can't win. From the age of six until I retired from racing, I competed to win. I prepared and planned to win. I surrounded myself with owners and crew members who wanted to win and were committed to being a winning team. We studied, we learned, we asked questions, we kept notes, and took videos. We bought the best equipment and we did the work in the shop and at the tracks so we would have the best chance possible to hit that mark. We did the "Ready" and the "Set" so that we could "Go!"

In the first eight chapters of this manual, I have shared some critical pieces for you to consider so that you can win at life. I pray God uses this manual as His tool and uses His Word to help get you to the next place. Let's call it "God's Garage!" It's here that you allow God to wash you, repair or replace some parts, and maybe do some fine tuning before

He fires you up and sends you back out. If God has done this in you, then you are prepared for the "ready" and "set" phase with God. Read on, my friend!

Part One
Ready?

Remember that famous quote by Tom Hanks in the movie *A League of Their Own*? "There's no crying in baseball!" But let me tell you, I've seen plenty of crying in baseball!

Back in the 1960s and '70s, most boys were taught that crying meant you weren't tough. I've already spoken of that monumental moment when, at the age of six, my mother left me all alone at 4:00 a.m. to go to work. From my second story bedroom window, I watched her back out of the carport and afterward, I cried myself to sleep. After that I fought to never cry again.

As a kid, I didn't cry when I lost at racing cars or motorcycles. I didn't cry when our small-town high school baseball team lost in the district finals after being rated number one in the state of Minnesota. Nope, other people cried in times like these, but not me.

But do you know where that hardness, that supposed toughness, eventually got me? To the pits of life. I finally decided to cry out to God because life was more than I could handle. After that, I cried every Sunday at church for four years straight. That was a different kind of crying. These were tears of joy because God had saved me and was healing my heart, week by week. He used both difficulties and joys to get me ready for the purpose He had already prepared for me.

Jett Fuel Moment

> Psalm 40:1–3 says, *"I waited patiently for the LORD; he turned to me and heard my cry. He lifted me out of the slimy pit, out of the mud and mire; he set my feet on a rock and gave me a firm place to stand. He put a new song in my mouth, a hymn of praise to our God. Many will see and fear the LORD and put their trust in him."*

When King David cried out to God, he was rescued and given a firm place to stand, singing a new hymn of praise to God. This was a witness to others so they could trust in the Lord as well. The following action points are based on what King David did in Psalm 40:1–3:

A. He cried out for help.

B. God heard and responded. 1 John 5:14–15 says, *"This is the confidence we have in approaching God: that if we ask anything according to his will, he hears us—whatever we ask—we know that we have what we asked of him."*

C. He was lifted out of the pit and placed on a rock.

D. He began to sing a new song (Psalm 40:3). There needs to be joy and singing God's praises when we are delivered from a pit, so others can know what He has done for us.

E. Many saw what God did and put their trust in Him. David was *ready*. He realized that God had answered his crying prayer and rescued him. He then began to sing praises to God everywhere. People heard his songs and wondered what he was singing about. David was celebrating his saving relationship with the living God.

Apply Psalm 40:1–3 and 1 John 5:14–15 to your life and situation today. Read King David's psalm, and as you do, try and recall what I've shared in the previous chapters so you can do what King David did. You can know God the way David did. And, my friend, once you are out of that pit, get ready!

Part Two
Set?

The moment you are placed on solid ground, your focus and attention need to change. You need to focus on the One who delivered you—God. The reason He pulled you out of the pit and put your feet on a rock is because He is always using His actions of love to reach many people. You need to:

A. Head for the One who saved you. Think about this: If you were rescued out of a literal pit, don't you think that you would track the person down who rescued you? Even in a literal sense, if another human saved you, wouldn't you quickly go and sincerely thank him? We should do the same thing when God rescues us. We need to run to Him and thank Him.

Don't be like Major Nelson on the television show "*I Dream of Jeannie*.[16] Jeannie was at Major Nelson's beck and call. Every time he got into trouble, he cried out for Jeannie, and she would deliver him. He would quickly thank her, and then he was off to his next thing. If God has delivered you, thank Him, praise Him, worship Him, and determine to know Him better.

B. Immediately begin to praise and worship Him. Don't just say, "Thanks, see you when I need you next time!" No, no, no! Now is the time to love Him back. Adore the Lord. And please realize, Jesus is worth having a relationship with for more than a minute. Keep your relationship with Him for the rest of your life, minute by minute by minute!

Jett Fuel Moment

> 1 John 5:3 says, *"This is love for God: to keep his commands. And his commands are not burdensome."*

King David says in Psalm 40:8, *"Your law is within my heart."*

Once God rescued King David, David loved God back. Something supernatural happened in that event. First, David recognized who God was. Second, he received a new heart through believing. And third, his heart began wanting to do things God's way.

Don't worry; when you commit your life to Christ, you'll still have a free will and can choose to live your own way—if that's what you want. Remember the old Burger King commercial that said, "Have it your way"?[17] God will let you have it your way but remember that He really does know what is best for us. He knows how to help us, so you might want to try it *His* way.

Then do what King David did in Psalm 40:

A. Offer your heart to God to be made pure, free from sin, and let it sing! Psalm 40:3: *"He put a new song in my mouth. A hymn of praise to our God."*

B. Trust God like never before. Psalm 40:4: *"Blessed is the man who makes the LORD his trust."*

C. Re-confirm your dedication to the Lord. Psalm 40:7: *"Then I said, 'Here I am. I have come.'"*

D. Determine to do God's will. Psalm 40:8: *"I desire to do your will, O my God."*

E. Determine to know God and His will by reading His Word (Bible). Psalm 40:8: *"Your law (Word/Bible, ways, will) is written on my heart."*

Take a deep breath and walk away from the things that led you away from God and walk toward Jesus.

Let's proceed to the final chapter and see what His purpose is for your new life. Ready? Set? Go!

CHAPTER 10

READY, SET, GO!

From sixth to eighth grade, my friend Steve and I rode our bicycles to school every day. Steve could practically ride a wheelie all the way to school, several streets long! I could do a wheelie for maybe a half a block. Steve loved *Dirt Bike* magazine and would bring the newest edition to school and show me how Roger Decoster and other world-famous motocross riders handled whoop-de-dos, corners with berms, and jumps. (My friend never knew that I was racing motorcycles as he was showing me these things! He never asked, so I never told him until much later.) Steve never raced, not even his bicycle. But he knew all about the sport from books and magazines.

Some people will never find out how awesome they could be because they never try anything new in life. Some are so good at racing in video games that they believe they would rule the world in a real race car. Unfortunately, this is not the way to move forward in life.

Whenever I talk about racing cars or motorcycles, people are interested. Some never found a way to try it, and others purchased cars or motorcycles but they seldom participated in races. We will never know how good they could be because they never went "go."

Sprint cars can only go forward; there is no reverse, and there's not even a transmission. They are push-started, and once they start, they go forward and fast!

We need to do the same thing in life.

If Jesus is your Savior and Lord, you have BE-come a new creation.

Out of that relationship with a new heart is a command to "DO" or "GO"!

Part of finding out God's will and purpose for your life is in the middle of the "go." Go where God is at work and join Him. "Go" is the third and equally vital piece of the process to know your purpose and win at life.

Ready, Set, Go!

Congratulations! You've made it to the final chapter. Maybe this is the place you initially wanted to flip to after picking up this manual. If you've read this manual from the beginning and have seriously pondered and received the Bible verses I've shared, then it might be time for a response. If you are already a Christian, maybe God the Holy Spirit has gotten your attention and led you to restore, refresh, or make right your relationship with Him. Maybe you're ready and able to hear His voice and respond to it. I pray you are ready to be delivered from a pit and seek His purpose for your life.

If you have never realized your need for a Savior, yet God has now revealed Himself to you by the power of the Holy Spirit, it's time to make a life changing decision. In simple humble recognition of who God is (and who you are not), you can confess your sins and ask Jesus to be your Savior. This is the first step to finding your God-given purpose in life.

GOD'S PURPOSE FOR YOUR LIFE

How do you find your purpose? By learning how to know, grow and go.

After reading this manual, some of you may be saying, "Come on, Jeff! I read all this way only to have you do the same thing the ads on Facebook do: "How to lose weight." "How to make a million dollars." Now you've wasted my time, Jeff. You aren't telling me what my purpose is in life. But you're telling *me* how to find it?"

Understand this: the Bible tells you God's purpose for your life. If finding your purpose is all you want to know, turn to the end of this chapter, and read the scriptures I've shared. But if you really want to see what your purpose looks like *lived out,* then keep reading!

By now you know that my dream, my plan "A," the purpose for my existence, in my opinion, was to be a professional race car driver. This dream came crashing down with my parents' divorce. Fast forward thirty years and the reality of that old childhood dream came back. I got the chance to race modified midgets and mini sprints. A few years later, I got to race sprint cars. I worked hard to land major sponsors so we could race sprint cars full time, rather than just the southwest tour we were part of. If this happened, part A and B of my dream would be fulfilled. But three attempts in three years to land a big sponsor were for naught.

Out of the blue, Patrick Sallaway, a fellow competitor who worked at Bondurant School of High Performance Driving, asked me to interview for a driving instructor position. I now shifted my dream to plan C, which was now looking really good. I was already racing sprint cars all over the Southwestern United States on weekends. If I worked at Bondurant during the week, I would get paid to train other drivers how to race and drive fast cars. At the same time, I would be honing my own driving skills in some of the best cars. I would be able to fly all over the country to privately train others as well. Could it get much better than this? I sure didn't think so.

I gladly agreed to the interview process. I arrived early and parked in the nearby empty casino parking lot. I began to pray. "God, you've been leading my life for the last five years. Please tell me what Your will is for this job."

God was faithful to speak. This is the only time I ever remember God giving me an option. He said, "I will bless you either way. Take the job or decline it." Wow! Don't you think I jumped at this opportunity?

Well, I didn't. During that time of my life, my relationship with my daughter had just been restored. Our first grandchild, Karson, had just turned one, and having him in my life was like getting a second chance at parenting the right way. We lived in the Verde Valley, two hours away from the driving school, which meant we would have to move to the Phoenix area. I couldn't stand the thought of being that far from my daughter and grandson.

Five years earlier there were things that had caused me to fall into the pits of life. My anger, temper, drinking, partying, and lust, to name a few, were things I wanted to leave behind. Even though I was a Jesus Geek, I knew that if I spent too much time around those former circles, I could be headed for a fall. Even though it seemed like a great opportunity, there were hidden risks.

I told God all I was feeling and going through. Naturally, He knew exactly what He was doing by giving me the choice. I went into that interview. The manager offered me the job—and I turned it down.

He asked, "Is it the money? I'll pay you more!"

"You don't have enough money to change my mind," I said. I shared my reasoning with him, but he still didn't understand.

You see, God's ways are not our ways. I turned down my dream, my plan, and what had been my purpose for existence. I turned down *good* for *best*—God's will. And I have never questioned it.

Two years later, God spoke to me again about my purpose and called me to become a pastor. Following His leading, I trained carefully, and pastored my first church in 2006. Since then, Deanna and I have pastored churches in four different states. Once I realized my purpose, I was literally taken from the pits to the pulpit.

Just as my race cars were created by the car builder, you and I are created by God, the builder of humans. He created us for a reason and with a purpose. The race car builder developed the cars by planning. In the same way, God made plans for us before we were born. Each of us has meaning. We are not mistakes. You were created by God with a purpose in mind.

Isaiah 49:1 says, "Before I was born the LORD called me; from my mother's womb he has spoken my name." And Psalm 139:13-14 says, "For you created my inmost being; you knit me together in my mother's womb. I praise you because I am fearfully and wonderfully made; your works are wonderful, I know that full well."

So, what is God's purpose for your life? Three words will help you find it: *know, grow,* and *go.* Tattoo these words on your brain.

Your first step after the pit—know, grow, and go. Your second step—know, grow, and go. For the next day, next week, and next year—know, grow, and go. You can know God's purpose in the moment, for a day, and for a season.

Know and *grow* is starting your morning in prayer with God. Know His Word, even if it's just a few verses you can meditate on so you can grow spiritually. Then ask Him to guide your day and to reveal to you your new purpose. Once you say "Amen," turn on your spiritual radar and go!

If you haven't heard God speak, just go where you know to go at this moment. If you're supposed to go to work today, then *go* to work. If you're an at-home parent, get up and *go* feed the kids before school. *Go* to the coffee shop. *Go* to the gym. *Go* where you ordinarily go.

Remember that attending a Bible-believing church regularly is part of know and grow. Become a part of the fellowship (race team), letting others hold you accountable, challenge you, and encourage you. Small groups, prayer groups, and mentors are also important as you know and grow.

God wants to use you in those regular places you go "out there." We are to be His light to the world, showing Christ-like character in our conduct and conversation. He also wants to use you "in there" in a local church. It is there that we learn how to serve God and serve others.

After I gave my life to the Lord, I went to work at my air-conditioning company, where I began living like Jesus in front of my employees. I lived it in front of my family and at the racetrack. These are the things I did as I began living a new life outside of the pits.

Dive into your purpose so much that you aren't worried about what you don't know yet. Dive in with Jesus to your current purpose and trust that He will get you where He wants you. As you walk and work with Jesus moment by moment, He may speak and take you to a new place or call you to prepare for a new position. Don't let pride stop you, no matter what God calls you to.

As pastors, God's purpose and plan for Deanna and I has taken us from pastoring full time in beautiful Sedona, Arizona, to the middle of nowhere in Terra Alta, West Virginia. We've lived with friends between jobs, and we've moved nine times in fourteen years. We were called to the coast in Newport, Oregon, moved over the mountains to Bend, Oregon, and from there went to Colorado. We have had plenty and we have had nothing. We've pastored and we've been janitors. If I were God, I would have done things differently! But God did it His way and accomplished eternal-value things. His purpose is always greater.

I've come to realize that going in God's plan and purpose for my life and being used by Him for kingdom purposes is simply the greatest. When I finally got my chance to race an 800-horsepower wing sprint car on the half mile track at Manzanita, it was the biggest adrenaline rush of my life. It was a "wow" moment! But the closer you get to God, the more you will have "wow" moments that far surpass my race car moment. My purpose and my moments now have eternal results. The race car experience didn't have eternal results. The cash and savings we make don't have eternal results. Toys and other possessions we acquire don't have eternal results.

Purpose is about people, all about people. The tools are the race cars, cash, savings, toys, possessions, places, positions, and everything else. And God uses the tools. Don't forget that. But the real purpose we have is about God and people.

Jett Fuel Moment

> Isaiah 43:7: *"Even every one that is called by my name: for I have created him for my glory, I have formed him; yea, I have made him"* (KJV).

> Psalm 100:2–3: *"Worship the Lord with gladness; come before him with joyful songs. Know that the Lord is God. It is he who made us, and we are his, we are his people, the sheep of his pasture."*

> In John 17:4, Jesus says, *"I have brought you glory on earth by completing the work you gave me to do."*

The Scriptures above show us that we were created for God's glory, giving Him praise through joyful worship. We were created to display God's glory with and through our lives, just like our example, Jesus Christ.

Know—Grow—Go

Successful race car teams have good cars and engines, good team members, good drivers, good equipment, and good tools. It's the same with God. We need good tools, such as a good study Bible in order to know, grow, and go.

One of the tools I use is a website called GotQuestions.org.[18] As I wrap this up, I'd like to share a commentary from this website entitled "The Purpose of Life."

> *"Our purpose in life, as God originally created man, is 1) glorify God and enjoy fellowship with Him, 2) have good relationships with others, 3) work, and 4) have dominion over the earth. But with man's fall into sin, fellowship with God is broken, relationships with others are strained, work seems to always be frustrating, and man struggles to maintain any semblance of dominion over nature. Only by restoring fellowship with God, through faith in Jesus Christ, can purpose in life be rediscovered."*

> *"The purpose of man is to glorify God and enjoy Him forever. We glorify God by loving, fearing, and obeying Him, keeping our eyes on our future home in heaven, and knowing Him intimately. We enjoy God by following His purpose for our lives, which enables us to experience true and lasting joy—the abundant life that He desires for us."*[19]

Know—Grow—Go ...
... and win at life.

John 14:6: *"Jesus answered, 'I am the way, the truth and the life.'"*

John 10:10: *"Jesus said, 'I have come that they may have life, and have it to the full.'"*

My prayer for all of you is that you would know God, grow in His likeness, and go tell others all He has done for you. That, my friends, is living life to the fullest.

Love ya,
Pastor Jeff

STEPS TO PEACE WITH GOD

By
Rev. Billy Graham

Simple steps to salvation by faith in Jesus Christ. From a booklet that the famous evangelist, Billy Graham, put together to simplify the salvation process. One that I have used countless times to lead people to salvation, a life-giving, peace-giving, eternal life-giving relationship with God. The booklet is called "Steps to Peace with God" (NKJV).

Step 1: God's Purpose—Peace and Life

God loves you and wants you to experience His peace and life-abundant and eternal. The Bible says:

> "We have peace with God through our Lord Jesus Christ" (Romans 5:1).

> "For God so loved the world that He gave His only begotten Son, that whoever believes in Him should not perish but have everlasting life" (John 3:16).

Why don't most people have this peace and abundant life God planned for us?

Step 2: The Problem—Our Separation from God

God created us in His image. He did not make us robots to automatically love and obey Him. God gave us a will and the freedom of choice; we choose to disobey Him and go our own willful way. This results in separation from God. The BIBLE says:

> "For all have sinned and fall short of the glory of God" (Romans 3:23).

> "For the wages of sin is death, but the gift of God is eternal life in Christ Jesus our Lord" (Romans 6:23).

People have tried many ways to bridge the gap between themselves and God. The Bible says:

> "There is a way that appears to be right, but in the end it leads to death." (Proverbs 14:12)

> "But your iniquities have separated you from your God; your sins have hidden his face from you, so that he will not hear." (Isaiah 59:2)

No bridge reaches God … except one.

Step 3: God's Bridge—The Cross

Jesus Christ died on the cross and rose from the grave. He paid the penalty for our sin and bridged the gap between God and people. The BIBLE says:

> "For there is one God and one mediator between God and mankind, the man Christ Jesus." (1 Timothy 2:5)

> "For Christ also suffered once for sins, the righteous for the unrighteous, to bring you to God." (1 Peter 3:18)

God has provided the only way. Each person must make a choice.

Step 4: Our Response—Receive Christ

We must trust Christ as Lord and Savior and receive Him by personal invitation. The BIBLE says:

> "Yet to all who did receive him, to those who believed in his name, he gave the right to become the children of God." (John 1:12)

"If you declare with your mouth, Jesus is Lord, and believe in your heart that God raised him from the dead, you will be saved." (Romans 10:9)

Which side are you on—the side with Christ—or without Him?

Here is how you can receive Christ:

1. ADMIT your spiritual need. "I am a sinner."
2. REPENT and be willing to turn from your sin.
3. BELIEVE that Jesus Christ died for you on the cross.
4. RECEIVE, through prayer, Jesus Christ into your heart and life.

CHRIST says, "Behold, I stand at the door and knock. If anyone hears My voice and opens the door, I will come in." (Revelation 3:20) The Bible also says, "Whoever calls upon the name of the Lord will be saved." (Romans 10:13)

What to Pray

Dear Lord Jesus, I know that I am a sinner and need Your forgiveness.

I believe that You died for my sins. I want to turn from my sins. I now invite You to come into my heart and life. I want to trust and follow You as Lord and Savior. In Jesus' name. Amen.[20]

Welcome to the family of God! By faith, you have just entered a life changing relationship with God the Father, God the Son, and God the Holy Spirit. (My first few chapters might make even more sense now!)

Romans 5:11 says, "Therefore, since we have been justified through faith, we have peace **with** God through our Lord Jesus Christ."

God has paved the way through Christ for us to have peace in our hearts. Take a few minutes and thank God for His love and for giving you a new life, a new heart, and peace like you've never experienced before. You now have the promise of eternal life with Him.

MY FAVORITE STUDY TOOLS

Life in the Spirit Study Bible

Favorite Bible translations: NLT and ESV

You Version Bible app

What the Bible Is All About, by Henrietta Mears

My Utmost for His Highest, devotional, by Oswald Chambers

Gotquestions.org

Blueletterbible.org

Billy Graham's, "Steps to Peace with God"

NOTES

Foreword
1. Jett Life Ministries, https://jettlife.org/services.

Chapter 1
2. Rev. Billy Graham, "Steps to Peace with God," https://memorial.billygraham.org/steps-to-peace/.

Chapter 3
3. Pete Seeger, "Turn, Turn, Turn," YouTube. Online video clip, https://www.youtube.com/watch?v=pKP4cfU28vM.

Chapter 4
4. Eckhart Tolle, "Eckhart Tolle and Oprah Winfrey: First Talk," YouTube. Online video clip, 2007, https://youtu.be/aj-t71IO6gA.

Chapter 5
5. Bondurant School of High Performance Driving, https://bondurantracingschool.com.

6. Robert Morris, "Staying in the Word, Three Steps to Victory," You Tube. Online video clip, https://youtu.be/zj-t71IO6gA.
7. MC Hammer, "U Can't Touch This," You Tube. Online video clip, https://youtu.be/_NNYI8VbFyY.

Chapter 6

8. Marlens, Neal (Creator), Black, Carol (Creator), & West, David John (Director) (TV Series 115 Episodes, 1988–1993), *The Wonder Years,* https://en.wikipedia.org/wiki/The_Wonder_Years, ABC Television.
9. Andy Williams, "Love is a Many Splendored Thing," YouTube. Online Video clip, https://www.youtube.com/watch?v=98pqW8h-sn4.
10. Nazareth, "Love Hurts Lyrics," YouTube. Online video clip, https://www.youtube.com/watch?v=6pHNkOQCIzk.
11. Lewis, C.S., "The Four Lives," (New York: Harcourt Brace, 1960.

Chapter 7

12. Mayo Clinic Staff, "Forgiveness: Letting Go of Grudges and Bitterness." https://www.mayoclinic.org/healthy-lifestyle/adult-health/in-depth/forgiveness/art-20047692, Nov. 13, 2020.
13. Stanton, Andrew; Peterson, Bob; Reynolds, David (Writers). Stanton, Andrew (Director) *Finding Nemo,* Pixar Animation Studios, Walt Disney, 2003.

NOTES

Chapter 8
14. Striker, Fran (Creator), Trendle, George W. (Creator), *Lone Ranger* (TV Series, 1949–1957.
15. Blackaby, Henry; Blackaby, Richard, King, Claude. "Experiencing God," (Nashville, TN, Lifeway Press, 2022).

Chapter 9
16. Sheldon, Sidney, *I Dream of Jeannie*, (TV Series, September 18, 1965–May 26, 1970, NBC).
17. Manilo, Barry (Writer). "Have It Your Way," YouTube. Online video clip, 1971. https://www.youtube.com/watch?v=CGj6jRGqT20.

Chapter 10
18. "The Purpose of Life," GotQuestions.org. https://www.gotquestions.org/purpose-of-life.html.
19. Rev. Billy Graham, "Steps to Peace with God," https://memorial.billygraham.org/steps-to-peace/.

CPSIA information can be obtained
at www.ICGtesting.com
Printed in the USA
BVHW041756160223
658686BV00012B/238